101 BEST

Web Sites

FOR

Kids

101 of the most **fun**, **educational**, and **interactive** Web sites for you and your child to enjoy!

Trevor B. Meers

Illustrator: Tony Caldwell

Publications International, Ltd.

Trevor B. Meers is an editor and columnist whose Web site reviews and articles about the Internet, World Wide Web, and online activities appear in various computer magazines and newspapers.

Check out the
Contents

What is the internet?

Learning about the Internet starts with one symbolic step: Looking around the room. It sounds pretty simple, but there's more to this than kids might think.

The room probably has some books sitting on a shelf. Maybe there's a TV over in the corner. There might even be a Nintendo or Sega system and cable stations hooked to the TV. The stereo sits quietly waiting for someone to listen. A poster of a famous sports player or musician might be hanging on one wall; maybe a picture somebody painted on another.

Then take a look out of the window. There are probably some busy animals, such as squirrels and birds, going about their business. A mailbox stands by the street—a street that leads out of the neighborhood and into the rest of the world.

Now come on back inside. Take a look at the computer. Everything just seen in the room and outside the house is in the computer—as long as the computer is connected to the World Wide Web (and the electrical socket . . .). The Web lets a computer connect to millions of other computers all around the planet. That means kids can sit at their desks and read stories, watch videos, look at pictures, play video games, learn about animals, talk to other kids, and visit just about any place they can think of. Using the Internet is like having a special ship that can travel anywhere on earth or in outer space. It even lets kids travel through time to learn about the past!

There's really no limit to what kids can find "online" (that's another word for using the Web). Even the experts who are developing the Internet don't know how far this cyber-world can go! All kinds of topics, discussed by people from all over the world, can be found by using the computer. Users meet lots of new friends online. There are about 56 million Americans online; that's more than 20 percent of the population!

And any kid can use the Web because the controls are really easy to learn. Anyone who knows how to use a computer already knows how to use the Web. To go online, users just have to point to pictures and buttons on the screen and click on them with the computer's mouse or track ball. Some Web sites get a little more complicated, but the people who run these sites are usually pretty good about explaining any new skills kids need to learn.

When kids use the Web, their computers get information from other computers all around the world. They talk to each other over the same telephone lines people use when they talk on the phone. That's why nobody in the house can make a phone call while someone else is using the Web. The computer's already on the phone talking to another computer! Parents can help set up the computer to make calls by hooking up a modem. Once it starts talking to other computers, kids can take over and start visiting Web sites. (Some parents might have had a separate phone line put in just for the computer so people can use the phone while kids cruise online.)

Web sites are like channels on the television. Users decide which Web site to look at just like they decide which TV channel to watch. But a TV might have only about ten channels. TVs hooked up to cable or a satellite dish can be tuned into anywhere from 30 to 100s of channels. Kids might think that's pretty impressive. However, although it's hard to pinpoint the exact numbers, there are probably about 200 million Web pages in existence!

Kids just tell the computer which Web site they want to look at by typing in an address like this: "http://www.nick.com." This tells the computer to call the Nick-elodeon computer and bring up its Web page. A lot of times visitors can just click buttons to change channels instead of typing in Web page addresses.

With so many Web sites to choose from, it's hard to decide where to visit. That's where we come in. *101 Best Web Sites for Kids* does just what its name says. It lists a bunch of cool sites for kids to check out. We've done most of the research and work so that kids will have a jump start on their Web activities. Look through the book for stuff that sounds cool, then start exploring. And a lot of the sites listed in this book also point to other worthwhile sites to visit.

It's time to get busy and explore the world through the computer! However, first we should discuss a few safety tips.

STAY SAFE
ON THE WEB.

Safety rules are a big part of life. Kids learn to look both ways before crossing a street. They know not to talk to strangers around town. But many kids may not know the safety rules for the

Internet. These tips are important to learn before going online. Surfing the Web without knowing how to be safe is as dumb as crossing a highway while wearing a blindfold!

All kinds of people use the Net. There are millions of nice people using the Net for all kinds of great things like those listed in this book. But there are also some bad people using the Internet, and some of them want to scare kids or even hurt them if they get a chance. Anyone can avoid the creeps and have a great time on the Web by following these simple rules:

* Kids should follow their parents' rules about when to go online and what kinds of things to do there.

* Kids shouldn't give their full names, ages, phone numbers, or street and e-mail addresses to anyone until they've asked their parents. Any passwords kids use should stay a secret, too.

* Nobody should put their picture online without asking their parents for permission.

* Sometimes people online say they'd like to meet in person. No way! Kids should never agree to meet anyone in person until their parents say it's OK and agree to go along to the meeting.

* The Internet lets people hide what they really look like, so it's easy for weirdos to lie about who they are. Smart kids don't believe what everyone says online.

* Surfing the Web should be a family activity so that sometimes Mom and Dad can see what kinds of things kids are doing online (and kids can see how their parents use the Web).

* If anyone online ever says something on a Web page, in e-mail, or in a chat room that makes a kid uncomfortable, they should leave

and quit talking to them. Then the kids should tell their parents what happened. Kids should never feel like it's their fault when someone else says something bad.

* Some programs have "viruses" in them. These viruses can make a computer sick, just like some viruses make people sick. Whenever users download a program from a Web site, they should use special antivirus software to scan files and make sure they're safe. Parents can make sure a computer has antivirus software.

By sticking to these rules, kids should enjoy the Web safely.

The picture to the right is an example of a Web browser. These programs have the tools that help guide kids around the Web.

Location bar: This is where users tell a computer what Web page

they want to see. Typing in a Web address such as "http://www.kids-com.com" tells the computer what Web page to visit.

Link: Text that is a different color and underlined, called a hypertext link, helps kids reach other Web pages. If a user points to it with the mouse arrow and the arrow turns to a pointing finger, users can click on the words to visit another Web page. The words

Netscape: Netcenter

Back Forward Home Reload Images Open Print Find Stop

Netsite: http://www.netscape.com/

Download WebMail

Netscape Netcenter

My Netscape Join Today!

Search the Web with Lycos [Search]
Classifieds Net Search Find Web Sites What's Cool What's New People Finder Yellow Pages

You've Got a Life. Now Get a Job. got name? Register www.Your-Name.com and recieve a FREE web page. Click Here! Only 2 Days Left to Enter the Silver Screen Sweeps

Contact : Address Book – Discussions – Instant Messenger – Long Distance – Members – WebMail

Autos
Buy a Car, Financing, SUVs...
Business
Careers, Small Business, News...
Computing & Internet
Free SW, News, Shops, Solutions...
Education
Colleges, Financial Aid, K–12...
Entertainment
Movies, Music, TV...
Games
Casino, Online Games...
Health
Diseases, Exercise, Women...
Kids & Family
Hobbies, Parents, Babies...

Local
Over 50 Cities, From NY to LA
Lifestyles
Food & Drink, Relationships...
Netscape
Products, Company, Developers...
News
Headlines, World, Tech...
Personal Finance
Investing, Taxes, Retirement...
Real Estate
Find a House, Remodel, Mortgage...
Shopping
Books, Music, Auctions, PCs...
Sports
Baseball, Golf, NFL...
Travel
Reservations, Flights...

Monday – October 5, 1998

Stock Quotes | Horoscopes
Sports News | Weather

ABCNEWS.com
• Impeachment Inquiry Proceedings Begin
• Nations Meet on Economic Woes
• Supreme Court Begins New Term
• Chat on Treating Heart Failure

Today Inside Netcenter
• Be smart. Try it before you buy it, in Software Depot.
• What are strong, powerful women saying when you're not around?
• Find the right car for you.
• Find your dream home in minutes.
• In-Box Direct: Free Magazines
• About Netcenter

explain what page the links go to. Sometimes pictures are links, too. Anything that turns the arrow into a finger is a link that, if clicked, will jump to another page.

Buttons: Click these buttons to visit a different Web page. The words explain what page the button will jump to. Buttons are the same as links.

Back button: This button goes back to the previous Web page. Clicking the Back button is like flipping backward through the pages of a book.

Forward button: If users have been using the back button, they can also use the forward button. Clicking the Back button brings up pages the user has seen before. Clicking the Forward button flips ahead again through the pages.

Scroll bar: Clicking the arrow on this bar moves a Web page up and down. When the whole page doesn't fit in the window, clicking the arrow at the bottom displays more of the page.

Favorites: This feature, which is sometimes called Bookmarks, makes it easy to visit favorite Web sites again and again. When users pull up this feature they see a list of Web sites. They can click the sites' names to go see them. This saves users from having to type in a Web page's address every time they want to visit it. Users can usually add a site they're looking at to this list by opening the Favorites, then clicking Add To Favorites.

Print button: Click this button to print the Web page on paper. Kids should make sure that it is legal to print pages from Web sites. Web page designers usually make it clear if it isn't all right to print a certain part of a page.

By Kids, for Kids

Most of the time, when something important gets built, it's built by adults. But on the Web, kids get their chance. Almost anybody can build a Web page with a little practice, so lots of kids build Web sites better than adults. Plus, there are a lot of sites that want kids to send in material such as stories and pictures. The sites in this section show off what kids are putting online.

Some kids go all out trying to help other kids with their sites. B.J. Pinchbeck is a good example. This hardworking kid lists all his favorite sites that will help kids do their homework. Some kids do their hard work away from the computer. Visitors learn about them at the Youth Hall Of Fame, which recognizes kids who serve their communities or put together great ideas that work.

Many of the sites in this section aren't built to provide help; they are looking for help. They want kids to be a part of the Web by sending in their artwork or stories. They'll post the material on the Web, making any kid a famous Web artist!

Kids are the best people in the world for knowing what kids like. The KIDS FIRST! site knows that's true, so it lets kids be the reviewers and write about their favorite videos and CD-ROM computer programs. This is the place to go to hear what everyone is talking about.

The kid reviewers look at videos and software that parents have picked as being kid-friendly (because they don't have bogus violence or bad language). The kids write what was good and bad about each product. Visitors start by clicking a category like "CD-ROM" or "Fairy Tales, Literature and Myth" from the site's map. In the product reviews, the line that reads "KIDS FIRST! KIDS SAY," shows where users can read what kids think of the title. They'll say what's good and not so good about the product and what ages it's for.

The site's Search button makes it easy to look up a specific video or program. It's a great tool for seeing what the kid jurors think of favorite products or for getting ideas for what to see next. Type in "Doug," for example, to see reviews of products with that goofy cartoon kid in them.

Kids sound off on videos and software

KIDS FIRST!

http://www.cqcm.org/kidsfirst/categf.htm

Don't take an adult's word for it. KIDS FIRST! lets kids do the talking by showing which products get a thumbs up from kid reviewers. Sometimes boys like a certain movie better than girls, or older kids like a CD-ROM better than younger ones. Kids First! says exactly who likes what in videos and computer programs.

Links:

* KIDS FIRST! Kids Corner
* Video Marketplace

A guide to sites for kids by a kid just like you

B.J. Pinchbeck's Homework Helper

http://tristate.pgh.net/~pinch13/

B.J. Pinchbeck can take a lot of the work out of homework. If kids need information about something like English, B.J. can point out tons of sites to check out. And he even narrows your search further by providing brief comments about the sites. He'll say which ones he likes with comments like "fun site to visit" and "wonderful collection."

Links:

* Search Tips
* Playtime
* Reference Section

Nobody knows what a drag homework can be better than a kid. So why not turn to another kid for help on getting that homework done? B.J. Pinchbeck helps students find the information they need to finish homework for any school subject. Students don't have to poke around the Internet for information because B.J. tells everyone exactly where to look for everything from simple dictionaries to online art galleries. His site has links to more than 450 great sites—and it's always growing.

On the main site page, the left side of the screen shows all kinds of school subjects. Click one such as Math, Science, or Social Studies for a list of sites that can help in that area. B.J. tells a little about each site so users know whether or not it sounds like something they would want to visit. A rotating "New" button, that looks like a coin in a Nintendo game, shows the new sites in the list, so it's easy to spot what's been added since the last visit. When someone in B.J.'s family really liked a site, he lets everyone know that, too.

And B.J. knows that there is more to life than homework. When it's time for a break from the books, the Playtime category on the left side of the screen suggests links to sites where kids can have some fun.

B.J. Pinchbeck's Homework Helper

Any kid who likes to write stories, poems, or anything else will dig The Young Writers Club, where any visitor can become one of the people writing the Web site. This is kids' big chance to get started as writers.

The Writers Club wants kids to send in as much writing as they can. There's even an award for the Member of the Year who sends in the most material. The club suggests ideas to help young authors get started by asking them to describe their scariest moments or to explain why certain songs are their favorites.

It's OK to just read what other kids say, too. The Club includes plenty of stories, movie reviews, opinions about things such as the Internet, and more. Check out the Global Wave magazine, which is written by kids. Special tips even help writers build their own Web pages.

Since this is a club, visitors get the chance to hang out with new friends. They can make key pals (online pen pals) and talk in chat sessions. Kids team up with each other to write a continuing story where everybody gets to add their ideas and make the story go wherever their imagination wants it to.

Young writers join this club by sending in their writing

THE YOUNG WRITERS CLUB

http://www.cs.bilkent.edu.tr/ ~david/derya/ywc.html

How many kids have ever written for a Web site before? They all can at this site. The Young Writers Club wants to know what kids think about things such as UFOs, the history of writing, and important people they know. Young authors can write their best stuff and send it in to be published on the Web.

Links:

* Word Of The Week
* Create Your Own Home Page
* Member's Stories and Poems
* Research Projects

The Young Writers Club

Meet some real-life kid heroes

YOUTH HALL OF FAME

http://www.youthhall.com/main.html

Trevor Farrel is a kid hero. When he was 11 years old, he saw on the news that lots of people didn't have any homes or food. He went to work to help them, and now he runs a special shelter called Trevor's Place where he helps homeless people. He's part of the group of kid heroes that get cyberspace kudos here at the Youth Hall of Fame.

Heroes don't have to be movie stars or sports champions. They don't even have to be adults! The Youth Hall of Fame shows off kids that could be the next hero to a lot of other kids. The members in this hall of fame are all between five and 18 years old. They've all done something great for their schools, communities, or friends and classmates in areas such as environmental action, the arts, and leadership.

This site has lots of ideas for projects visitors can try around their own school or town. Kids learn about Kelly Moser, for example. She's only 12 years old, but her business creating friendship-pin flags is such a big hit that she's even sent them to President Clinton. Remember that kids in this hall of fame are just regular people. Any kid can do important work just like these kids are—just come up with a good idea and go with it! This site tells how to start a Youth Hall of Fame in any area to encourage local kid heroes.

Visitors who know a kid who's done something awesome can team up with the kid's parents to send his or her name into the Youth Hall of Fame. That special friend could get into the Hall and become another kid hero!

What makes a GreatKid? Being great takes a lot of special qualities, but the biggest one is knowing that: "Doing nice things for other people makes us feel good about ourselves." That's the whole idea behind the GreatKids Network, a site dedicated to honoring kids who go out of their way to help others. The kids described in the GreatKids stories show others that they, too, can make a difference with a little work. The young folks here are real examples to other kids.

The Stars and Co-stars sections tell all about different GreatKids. Jamie, for example, started food drives to help hungry people when she was nine. Now she's helped hundreds of hungry people and has become a star in newspapers and on TV—all because she wanted to help other people! Eric started using his amazing musical talent to teach other kids music when he was in seventh grade. Now whole crowds of kids play instruments thanks to Eric. Other GreatKids clean up neighborhoods, write mystery stories, and invent machines.

Anybody who works to do great things can be part of the GreatKids network. A special Speak Up section lets kids write in about things they've done lately for others that made them feel good.

Young stars show how helping others makes kids feel great

GreatKids Network

http://www.greatkids.com

Any kid can become a GreatKid when they look for ways to help others. The stars at this site have creative ideas for making a difference around the neighborhood. The Web site even helps kids find organizations that need their help in helping others.

GreatKids Network

Online show-and-tell of the best kids' work in every subject

KIDS DID THIS!

http://sln.fi.edu/tfi/hotlists/ kids.html

It doesn't take an adult expert to explain how planes fly. Stuart and Daniel are from Heronsgate Middle School. They prove that they're up on this topic on their science project Web page. And they just love kids to visit them for the information. Their project and a lot more are waiting in the Kids Did This! collection.

Links:

* Educational Hotlists
* Electronic Elementary Magazine

Looking at projects made by other kids is great for a couple of reasons. When kids compare work, they can see how their own projects stack up against the competition, and they can get new ideas for their next school assignments and hobbies. The Kids Did This! Web site helps in both cases by gathering together a big group of projects from kids around the world. It's like a science fair, art show, and speech contest all rolled into one.

Visitors start by selecting a category such as science, social studies, art, mathematics, or school newspapers. Clicking a category shows a list of all the kid-made projects inside. Some of the categories have 50 or more projects to look at. There are some great topics here such as the stamps kids drew to honor Native Americans. Some of the kids' projects are activities like the Where Are You? quiz that makes players guess where the kids live. A few kids have posted sites telling all about their schools and hometowns.

Remember that this site is mostly about fun stuff. These projects aren't from experts. Before anyone uses information in the reports for school projects, they should first check the facts.

Legend says that there's a pot of gold at the end of the rainbow. The treasure at the end of the Reading Rainbow may not be shiny gold, but it can be just as exciting to find. The Reading Rainbow is famous for introducing kids to entertaining stories to read. The Rainbow's Young Writer Contest gets kids into stories even more—by writing the stories! The stories here are the best ones kids sent in to the writing contest. Visitors can read the stories that won the grand prize, plus one or two runner-up stories in each category.

These kid authors are really into it. Each writer illustrates the stories with their own pictures, which make every story seem to jump right off your computer screen. These talented authors might even give kids some ideas for stories of their own!

Some of the winning stories are made-up tales, like the "The Computer That Wished It Could Walk" by kindergartner Sanjay Saverimuttu. Others are true tales about how the kid authors live. First-grader Mary Gage talks about helping her dad get sugar from trees. Aurora Johnson won a prize for her poetry about the natural beauty all around her Alaskan home.

Read all kinds of stories from prize-winning kid authors

READING RAINBOW
YOUNG WRITER CONTEST WINNERS

http://www.pbs.org/ readingrainbow/index.html

It's hard to decide what to be as a grown-up. You might be able to write your own ticket as an author. The stories at this site show how well kids can write. There are amazing stories hiding inside every kid's head. Kids can take a look at these tales and, who knows, they might even get a story idea of their own!

Reading Rainbow

This online art gallery shows only kids' work

GLOBAL CHILDREN'S ART GALLERY

http://www.naturalchild.com/gallery/

Kids in other countries are a lot like kids in America in some ways. That's easy to see in the pictures they draw. Sang-Woo Y. from South Korea is six and likes to draw fruit. Another six-year-old, Sharnee M. from Australia, draws owls and cats. The gallery shows all kinds of work from kids all over the world and even displays the flags of their countries.

A lot of parents hang pictures their kids create on the family refrigerator. But it would take a gigantic refrigerator to hold pictures drawn by kids from all over the world. Since nobody has a fridge that big, there are Web sites like the Global Children's Art Gallery. It's the place where all kinds of kids can hang their pictures for the world to see.

Tons of drawings are displayed here from kids living in countries such as Korea, Canada, Australia, and even right here in the United States. The Art Gallery lists the name of each picture. Some are funny like "Devon's Wooly" or "Galah!" Some picture names are adventurous like the dinosaur picture called "Belosyreptor" from Yoon-Jong S. from South Korea. Kids can click any picture to see a bigger version of it. Anybody who likes one of the pictures can use the Print button on the screen to print it out.

Of course, a lot of young Web users can probably draw as well as these kids. The Global Children's Art Gallery would love to make new drawings part of the show. Any kid 12 years old or under can send in a picture to go on the Web site.

A person's name isn't just another word. It tells everybody who they are. Plus, after a little searching, people can discover that their names have secret meanings. Edward, for example, means "rich guardian." Other names, such as those for days, months, and even pets, mean things, too. The kids and adults who built the What's in a Name? site can help anyone learn what all these names mean.

The search starts with a click on a link for a category of names such as First Names. There's a big list of boys' and girls' first names from Albert and Amanda to Whitney and William. The site's creators included a little history of each name. Who would have guessed the name Tiffany comes from the country of Greece? The Last Names section lists the 25 most common last names in America. Kids can look for their last names on the list. The section on Famous Name Changers tells about folks who decided they wanted new names.

The Days section tells how important the Vikings and Romans were to the words people use today. These people from a long time ago named every day on our calendar. Kids can talk like a Viking if they call Thursday "Thor's Day" instead.

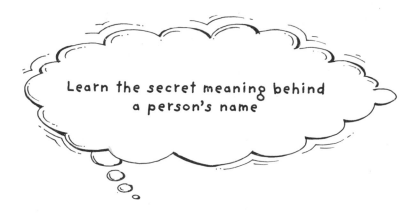

Learn the secret meaning behind a person's name

WHAT'S IN A NAME?

http://tqjunior.advanced.org/4626/

Reebok sneakers might make athletes run as fast as a gazelle. After all, Reeboks are named after gazelles, which look like deer and run fast. Nike shoes are named after a goddess of victory, so maybe they'll help their owners win! Adidas shoes have a more traditional name; they're named after Adi Dassler, who makes them.

Links:

* Pet Names
* About This Site
* Requests From Guests

Enter this art contest or just check out other kids' stuff

SUPER'S STUDIO

http://www.ponyshow.com/ KidsNet/studio/studio.htm

Tenzin lives far away in the mountains of India. The school there is poor, but Tenzin still is one of the prize-winning kid artists at Super's Studio. Tenzin is just one of the interesting kids featured in this Web art gallery. Kids can send in their art, and maybe they'll win!

Artists work hard in their studios. That's where they concentrate on making their paintings and other works as good as possible. Kid artists are hard at work in Super's Studio. This site is a place to see the great drawings that kids send in. Visitors can even meet the artists and send in their own drawings to the art contest.

The Prize Pictures link shows off the kinds of drawings that win the prizes in Super's contests. The drawings of things like trains and monsters from kids such as Marty and Sara are really good! The Meet The Artist! links tell more about the kids who sent the pictures. Six-year-old Sara made her picture with a graphic design computer program and she loves to read and swim.

Super's Studio is about more than just looking at other kids' pictures, though. Kids can draw their own creations and send them to Super's Studio. The best pictures will show up on this Web site, and the winners will appear in the Meet The Artist! section. That means if a kid's picture is a good one, they can become a star on the Web!

Homework Helpers

Homework assignments would be a breeze if kids had an expert on every subject living in their home. They could provide tips on tough math problems, talk all about the planets in our solar system, or help with any other subject. However, most people probably don't have anyone that smart hanging around. In fact, there probably isn't one person anywhere who's an expert on everything.

Knowing how to use the Web provides access to all kinds of experts. The sites in this section are great for helping kids finish hard assignments whenever they get stuck. Kids can think of the Web as a huge, easy-to-use reference book.

But unlike books, the Web can talk back to kids. (Well, sort of.) Kids can send questions to experts all over the world through e-mail. Then the experts will write back to kids with answers to tough questions, making kids feel like real homework research pros. Some of the sites in this section even let kids have some fun while they learn. Kids might even turn studying into something they actually like doing!

The place to learn about famous folks

BIOGRAPHY.COM

http://www.biography.com/find/find.html

Biographies cover lots of people besides just the names in history books. Try looking up some of kids' favorite names like Dr. Seuss. They'll find out that the doctor's real name is Theodor Seuss Geisel. Of course, historical facts are pretty interesting, too. For instance, kids can find out that when George Washington's dad died, George had to go live with his older brother.

Links:

* HistoryChannel.com
* Biography television schedule

Biography.com knows when Teddy Roosevelt was born. It knows where Florence Nightingale grew up. It even knows where President Clinton went to college. In fact, Biography.com can tell kids all about the life of almost any famous person. No matter who they need to learn about, chances are, they'll find them here. This site is a great resource when writing papers or doing other homework about famous people for school.

Just click the Find button on the main page and type in the name of the person. That person's name then pops up on a list. Click their name to read their life story. Biography.com tells kids why these important people are famous, important dates in their lives, and what other famous people they worked with or knew. Kids might even be able to click other names in the story to read the biographies of those folks, too (look for any underlined links). Remember that lots of living people are covered at Biography.com. Look up names such as Michael Jordan to learn more about current celebrities.

Biography.com

No question is too hard or too simple for Dr. Math. This wizard of numbers will answer almost any math question kids send in through e-mail. Sometimes he answers beginner questions like "Does 1 + 1 make 2 or 11?" Other times, he tackles harder topics like explaining commutative and inverse properties. No matter what the topic, his answers are always clear enough to help kids do better in math class.

All the homework help at The Math Forum Student Center can help students do better on the next big math exam. Click Elementary on the main page to get information especially for kids from ages 5 to 11. When kids have a specific problem to solve, go straight to Ask Dr. Math. If they're just looking for ways to brush up on skills, they can try different exercises around the site.

The Math Tips & Tricks are especially handy. These secrets teach kids to do math faster than a calculator. Tips here explain fast ways to multiply by 9 or 5 and how to decide what numbers are divisible by 3. With practice, kids can turn into real math masters with these expert ideas.

The features here add up to math-mania!

THE MATH FORUM STUDENT CENTER

http://forum.swarthmore.edu/ students/

Take a math quiz with a set of electronic flash cards. The Math Forum's Quick Reference Section connects to a site called A+ Math that asks math questions and immediately lets kids know if the answers are right. Kids decide how hard the questions are and what type of mathematics they want to practice.

Get involved while exploring science

EXPLORATORIUM EXPLORANET

http://www.exploratorium.edu/

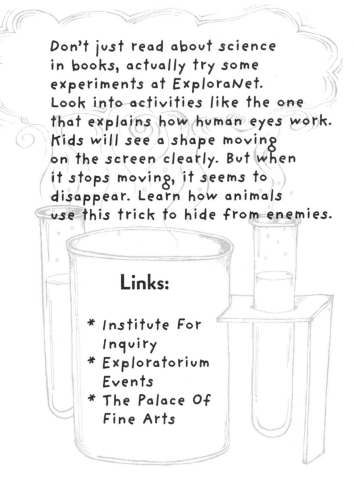

Don't just read about science in books, actually try some experiments at ExploraNet. Look into activities like the one that explains how human eyes work. Kids will see a shape moving on the screen clearly. But when it stops moving, it seems to disappear. Learn how animals use this trick to hide from enemies.

Links:

* Institute For Inquiry
* Exploratorium Events
* The Palace Of Fine Arts

If actually trying something sounds better than listening to someone talk about it, take a look at ExploraNet. This site for curious kids is based on the Exploratorium museum in San Francisco where visitors get to dig into science experiments. ExploraNet puts some of the best science exhibits and experiments online for kids to try.

Visit some of the Exploratorium's great exhibits in The Digital Library. A few explain why people's eyes play tricks on them. Also, there are some audio files that show how the way kids speak can be just as important when communicating as the words that are said.

The Learning Studio's Science Explorer section is packed with science activities for kids to try. Learn how to mix a solution that turns dingy, old pennies shiny. Read the instructions for growing crystals in a bowl on a sunny shelf.

Special features explore areas like the shape of rocks in Death Valley National Park and how people's feet are the greatest piece of sports equipment. Or, for those kids who are not easily grossed out, follow along as a scientist dissects a real cow eyeball!

Famous art might seem kind of boring. After all, they're just pictures right? But when kids know what to look for, every painting has some secrets to tell. Kids will have to listen to those secrets to solve cases when they play A. Pintura Art Detective. After finishing this adventure, designed for kids in fourth grade and up, they'll never look at "pictures" the same way again.

Fiona Featherduster has come for help in identifying a mysterious painting found in her grandfather's attic. She knows one of the six famous artists on her list painted it, but kids need to figure out which one. Artist names such as Raphael and Picasso may not mean much now, but kids will learn what each painter was known for as the case goes on. Picasso made over 20,000 paintings, but do the Picasso paintings on the Web page look like the mystery painting? Make a guess and see if Fiona thinks it is right.

By the end, kids will be able to match paintings with the artist that made them. They will even identify the mystery painting! Children will now like looking at famous art because they will understand secrets like composition and color to study in each painting.

Brush-up on art knowledge and solve the big case

A. PINTURA ART DETECTIVE

http://www.eduweb.com/pintura/

Want someone to paint a picture of dad mowing the lawn? What artist would do the best job? After kids become "A. Pintura Art Detective," they'll know that Millet would be the man. He was famous for realistic paintings of people at work. Follow Pintura's case to learn other art facts.

Links:

* Inside Art
* Educational Web Adventures

A. Pintura Art Detective

Quick facts are just a few clicks away

ENCYCLOPEDIA.COM

http://www.encyclopedia.com

It only takes a few seconds to catch up to one of the fastest men in history. Just click the Y book and find Chuck Yeager's name. Kids will learn that he was the first person to fly faster than the speed of sound. Kids will find this kind of quick information on almost any topic at Encyclopedia.com

Links:

* Infonautics
* Related Internet Sites
* Related Books at BarnesandNoble.com

It would take a shelfful of books to hold all the information that kids can pull up on the computer screen when visiting Encyclopedia.com. This site lets kids read the articles in a whole set of encyclopedias without ever opening a book. The 17,000 articles here tell children about almost any topic they can come up with. When just getting started on a topic, look here for the basics (for example, to find out when George Washington Carver was born).

To start a search, just point to the book on the shelf that has the letter of the subject in question. For example, when looking for information about President Abraham Lincoln, click the L book, then look through the list to find Abraham Lincoln's name. Click it to read a short article about this great man. Use the links to visit other sites packed with more information on related topics.

Kids can do the same thing to look up articles about everything from apes to zoology. Or, to avoid just browsing around, go right to the topic by using the Search window on the main page. Type in the desired topic and click Find It! for a list of articles to read.

Here's where to find help on almost any topic. The big Study Web site rounds up all kinds of sites and sticks them in categories. That makes it easy for kids to quickly find the help they need.

Let's say a teacher asked for students to find out where computers came from. Go to Study Web and click Computer Science. Then click History Of Computers. A big list of sites with information in that area will then pop up on the screen. Choose "A History Of Computers In The '70s, '80s, '90s" or another site. Kids could also pick something like Animals & Pets, then choose Endangered Species, and then Alligators. A search tool lets kids type in the words they're looking for and jump right to them.

Study Web tells children a little about each site so it's easy to pick the best one. It ranks each Web site for a grade level, such as "5 +." That means it's for any kid in fifth grade or higher. However, as with most anything on the Web, visit any site that looks interesting.

Be sure to try the Study Buddy link. This helpful resource provides a little reference window with a dictionary, thesaurus, calculator, and more.

Where to find help for any homework assignment

STUDY WEB

http://www.studyweb.com/

It's easy to do homework well when kids know where to go for help. Study Web tells kids where to find information all over the Web. Just click a category, such as History, Music, or Science, to see the best sites in those categories.

Links:

* The Parent Education Ring
* TeacherNet
* The Classroom Internet

Study Web

Explore earth's outer space neighbors

THE NINE PLANETS

http://www.ex.ac.uk/tnp/

The computer becomes a spaceship and helps kids travel throughout the solar system at this site. Click the section for Mars, a planet close to Earth, and see pictures of rocks taken as recently as 1997. Learn facts like how the month of March is named after the planet Mars.

Links:

* Master Picture List
* MarsWatch
* NASA Spacelink
* The Planetary Society

Don't blast off into an outer space homework assignment without voyaging to The Nine Planets. This site tells kids all about planets in our solar system, along with other things zipping around out there like asteroids, moons, and comets. The site's writing is geared toward older elementary kids, but anyone can enjoy the out-of-this-world photos and helpful links to other information.

Click each planet's name to get the basics about it such as its size and surface temperature. (This is a metric site and lists measurements in kilometers and kilograms.) Kids will also read the stories of humans discovering and exploring each planet. The planet Pluto, for example, isn't named after a cartoon dog. It's named after a Roman god that supposedly lived in the underworld. This planet is so far from the sun's light that it reminded people of that mythological god. Use links to learn about spacecrafts that have visited the planets.

A glossary explains spacey words such as "astronomical unit" and many others so kids will never be confused. Some sections explain subjects like how planets and other space objects (moons, satellites, etc.) get their names and what mystery planets may still be undiscovered in space.

There's a lot more to geography than finding states on the map. Winners at this site's games will know about maps around the world and something about the earth's water, land, and animals.

Click Enter Geo-Globe on the main page to reach a list of the site's six games. They all use maps and pictures to test kids' knowledge of a different geographical area. In Geo-Find, kids name the locations of cities, countries, rivers, and mountains. Start with the beginner level because the other questions get pretty hard! (Like asking kids to locate Lesotho.)

Geo-Globe also lets children explore other parts of the globe. Geo-Quest lets kids guess the name of a mystery animal. Get clues by asking questions about where the animal lives and how big it is. Geo-Seas covers the oceans. Geo-Tour has kids follow clues to find famous landmarks. There are several other sections as well.

Funny sounds let kids know whether their answers are wrong or right, and links help them look up the answers they don't know right away. Even when kids get some answers wrong, Geo-Globe makes it easy to learn from their mistakes.

Learn geography and more while playing games

GEO-GLOBE: INTERACTIVE GEOGRAPHY

http://library.advanced.org/ 10157/

Finding a town on the map of the United States is pretty easy. OK, now try pointing to Ethiopia on a map of the world. That's something kids will have to do when they play a game of Geo-Find. They'll also have to point out places such as Iceland and Mexico.

Geo-Globe: Interactive Geography

Money is what makes this site go 'round

KIDSBANK.COM

http://www.kidsbank.com/index_2.html

Ever wonder where pennies come from? Penny the coin can tell kids all about it. Money starts out as a big piece of metal at a place called the U.S. Mint. The workers stamp out pennies just like cookies, then send them first to a Federal Reserve Bank, and then to banks all over. Eventually (if the chores have been done!), they end up in kids' piggy banks, waiting to be spent on whatever their hearts desire!

Adults talk about money a lot, so it might seem like something that kids don't want to mess with. But money's important to everybody. Lots of kids earn money through allowances, lemonade stands, mowing lawns, or doing other jobs. Learning about money helps kids buy more with the money they have.

KidsBank.Com helps young folks learn the basics of how money and banks work. Cartoon characters such as Penny and Dollar Bill take users on tours of various money topics. Start with Penny because she explains important questions such as why we have money, who makes new coins and paper money, and whose pictures are on paper money. The information about bank topics such as earning interest is best for older kids. Whenever the Professor appears, click him for more in-depth lessons.

Kids can head to the game room to test how much they've learned, and use calculators to figure out how long it takes to become a millionaire. Send money questions to Mr. Money. He'll post an answer in a couple of days, and kids can read answers to other people's questions about topics such as credit cards and savings accounts.

When kids visit a big city, they need a friend to show them around. The Internet has more people on it than any big city, so people need a friend to give them directions there, too. Ask Jeeves for help. This friendly butler lets kids ask questions in any words they want. He'll look around the Internet and show them where to find the answer.

Ask Jeeves for Kids is a search engine. That means it's a tool that can tell kids where to find everything on the Web. Ask Jeeves is easy for kids to use because they can type in their question just like it comes into their head. Ask Jeeves, "How old is the moon?" and he'll show you questions he can answer on that topic such as "Where can I find general information on the moon?" Click one of the questions to visit a site that has the answer. Jeeves does all the work and delivers the answer, acting just like kids' own personal librarian.

Check Jeeves' Question Of The Day to see how he answers a typical question. Check out the Conquer the Web with Jeeves section to get great information about creating Web pages and to find some online games.

A friend who understands kids and has the answers

ASK JEEVES FOR KIDS

http://www.ajkids.com

Jeeves can answer almost any question about what's on the Web. Kids can even ask in their own words. Ask Jeeves, "Where are the hoops scores?" and he'll tell kids where to look for college, NBA, and WNBA basketball scores. Jeeves is a cool Web searcher who understands how kids talk.

Ask Jeeves for Kids

Get to know the U.S. presidents

A PRESIDENTIAL EXPLORATION

http://library.advanced.org/ 11492/index2.html

It's tough to become a U.S. president. Andrew Jackson got more votes than his opponent in 1824's big election, but he still didn't get the job. That's one of the weird things that can happen in our voting system for this important job. Check out the details in the Convention section of this site.

One job in America is so tough to get that only 41 men have ever done it (one man did it at two different times in history), even though our country is over 220 years old. Being the U.S. President is a special job, and kids can find out what it's like at A Presidential Exploration.

Use the Oval Office link to look up information on a certain president. Each section tells kids what happened to a president while he was in office and lists what he did while he had the job.

The Convention link teaches what it takes to be president. First, a potential president must be at least 35 years old. Then they have to get people to vote for them in an election. Kids will also learn that the president has a lot of power, but he can't just do anything he wants. Learn the rules every president has to follow.

When kids get tired of studying, they can have fun with their presidential knowledge in the Rec. Room. Four games here test how much kids know about presidential facts and pictures. The Presidents Quiz is the easiest one. Tackle multiple-choice questions such as, "Which president is known as the 'Father of his country'?"

Practicing math is important, but it sure can get boring. The next time kids need to practice addition, subtraction, or other math, they can try playing baseball instead. Funbrain.com Math Baseball lets kids play a game at the same time they're practicing math.

When kids show up at this ballpark, they can just pick the math skills they need to work on. Practice one task, such as multiplication, or several math skills at once. Then choose a skill level from easy, medium, hard, or super brain. The pitcher throws a math problem at kids like "6 × 5 =" and if they answer it right, they'll get a single, double, triple, or home run depending on how hard the question was. Children will see their base runner heading around the bases. Kids are out if they miss a question. Kids might have such a good time playing baseball, that they'll wind up practicing their math skills more than ever before.

Funbrain helps kids practice other skills, too. Check out the "Click Here For More Games" link. Play Spell Check and spot the misspelled words. If kids see enough misspellings, they'll get to put their name on the leader board.

Do the math to take a swing at this baseball site

FUNBRAIN.COM MATH BASEBALL

http://www.funbrain.com/math/index.html

Get a bat ready and keep an eye on the pitch.... Here it comes: "8+7= ?" Take a swing by answering "15." That's right! And now a runner is heading to third base. That's how to play Funbrain.com Math Baseball, and that's how kids have fun practicing math.

Links:

* More Games
* Sites Made by Kids

Learn the secrets of super students

THE LOONEY BIN

http://www.geocities.com/Athens/3843/index.html

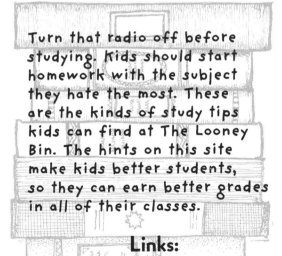

Turn that radio off before studying. Kids should start homework with the subject they hate the most. These are the kinds of study tips kids can find at The Looney Bin. The hints on this site make kids better students, so they can earn better grades in all of their classes.

Links:

* Improve Your Study Skills
* Taking Good Notes

School isn't just about studying reading, arithmetic, and other class subjects. A big part of school is studying to be a better student. When kids get good at things such as taking notes and doing homework, they'll do great all through school. The Looney Bin site helps kids become great students.

The Looney Bin is probably best for older elementary school kids. Those students need to learn note taking, study habits, report writing, and other skills to get them ready for middle school and high school. But even little kids can check this site out for better ways to do their homework.

Start by taking the "Are You A Good Student?" quiz. It helps kids decide where they need to improve their study skills. Then kids can use the tips on the page to work on those areas. For example, kids will learn to start their homework when they first get home from school and to tackle the hardest subject first. Learn key words for report writing such as "first draft" and "outline." Kids can even get more courage for taking tests with the site's advice for handling tough questions. They can just think of every test as a chance to show their stuff.

Nobody can be an expert in everything. Children just have to find the real experts and ask them questions. Try sending questions through the Web to a professional in any field. It's like a big room full of smart people waiting to help kids.

The Ask an Expert Sources page puts kids in touch with all kinds of smart people. Kids can find help on subjects such as Math, Dinosaurs, Health, and Native American Culture. They'll talk to people such as Dr. Math and Dr. Bug. The experts come from all over, so their rules for answering questions may all be different. Some will write back to kids personally. Some will put the answer on a Web page. A lot of the experts list answers to the questions they get most. An answer may already be listed inside.

Make the expert's job easy when sending in a question. Kids can tell the experts their age and where they've already looked for information. Ask a specific question like, "Where do whales spend the winter?" instead of "Tell me about whales." This helps the experts answer questions clearly.

Remember: These experts aren't here to do kids' homework. Kids should only ask for help after looking for information themselves first.

All kinds of experts help kids with hard questions

ASK AN EXPERT SOURCES

http://www.cln.org/int_expert.html

Kids can get a NASA scientist, a doctor, and Dino Russ the dinosaur expert to help them with their homework this week. These experts—and a whole bunch of others—are waiting to answer questions kids send in through e-mail. They can tell kids everything from what the biggest dinosaur was to why diamonds cost so much.

Everything gross and gooey is explained here

THE YUCKIEST SITE ON THE INTERNET— YOUR GROSS & COOL BODY

http://www.yucky.com/

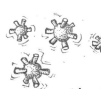

Maybe the teacher won't talk about boogers, but this Web site will. Kids can click the names of body parts to learn about things they might be embarrassed to ask a real person about. This site has the answers about all the gross things going on inside of people's bodies.

Some weird things happen inside people's bodies. Bumpy, gurgling sounds rumble deep in their stomachs. Sometimes bad breath scares everybody away. Then there's the gross stuff kids don't even talk about. These are normal body actions, and kids have a right to know why they happen. The Yuckiest Site on the Internet tells kids why all this stuff is going on.

Move the pointer over the list of topics next to Dora's picture. Kids can learn about whatever body part they want by aiming the pointer at the name of that feature. Click "Stinky Pits" to learn why armpits stink sometimes. Kids will learn where all kinds of gross stuff comes from, including dandruff, belches, and hiccups. Sections on each body part let kids get the answers to questions like "Why do we vomit?" (also called throwing up or barfing) and "Why is vomit green?" Fun Facts tell kids more about things like how flies use vomit to eat. Wendell the Worm, an ace reporter, answers any questions kids send in.

The Yuckiest Site on the Internet can explain about all kinds of stuff. There are special sections on bugs and even worms. Kids can read about parasites called tapeworms that live inside of animals—and even people sometimes!

No really tough homework question can stump kids when they use a personal homework helper. Send questions to real-life teachers at the Homework Help site who know about every school subject. They'll read kids' questions and send answers back.

Some answers are long; some just tell kids where to look for answers. It depends on the teacher answering the question. Don't count on this site for help the night before a report's due. Kids will probably have to wait about 24 hours or longer for the answer. Make this a study tool, but not the only tool.

Click Elementary School Topics. Then go to the bottom of the page and click the Search button. Kids can type in the topic they need help on, like "Christopher Columbus" or "snakes." They might find answers teachers have already given other kids on the same topic. If the search doesn't help, kids can click a subject name on the left side of the screen, then keep choosing subjects until they find the right one. Then, questions and answers will appear.

If kids want to ask their own question, go to the bottom of the screen and click Add Discussion. Start looking for the teacher's answer the next day.

Teachers help kids at home at this site

HOMEWORK HELP

http://www.startribune.com/ stonline/html/special/homework/

"Help! No one knows the answer to my question!" When kids feel that way, they can jump on the Homework Help site. Even if kids need an answer to a question as weird as "Why do geese fly in the shape of a V?" a real teacher can help them find the answer.

Links:

* Information Please
* Adler Planetarium and Museum
* the WebMuseum

See what important events happened on any date

THIS DAY IN HISTORY

http://www.historychannel.com/today/

Kids know that July 4 is an important date in history. However, a lot more has happened on July 4 than Independence Day in the United States. Calvin Coolidge, the 30th president of the United States was born on July 4, 1872. A U.S. zoo had its first baby king cobra snakes on that date in 1955. Check out what else has happened on that important day.

Links:

* The History Channel
* Great Speeches
* History Fun & Games
* History Store

It's hard to imagine what life was like way back in history. It might be easier to think about one day in history, maybe today's date in . . . 1776 or 1950. This Day in History shows children what important things happened on this very day throughout history.

When kids visit the site, one major event that happened on the curent date is right at the top. There's usually a movie or audio clip to go with that event. Click a button to see what happened on this day in other years and a list of famous people born on this day. There are even lists of songs that were big hits on this day. Kids can check to see how many they have heard of before.

The coolest part about this site is that kids can look up any day to see what happened in history. Users can look up their birthday and see the events listed there. They can also check what famous people have their birthday. When working on a school history project, kids can look up the day they're writing about and add that extra information to their report. Kids may know that the Declaration of Independence was approved on July 4, 1776, but what else has happened on that day throughout history?

Kids should read FAQs whenever they see them. "FAQs," which stands for Frequently Asked Questions, answer questions most users have. There's a good chance that if kids are wondering about something, it's explained in FAQs. The KidsConnect FAQs answer homework questions kids have most often. The answers come from professional librarians.

KidsConnect groups the FAQs by subject. In the subjects, choose from areas such as history, science, news, and animals. Click a subject to see questions such as "Why do leaves change colors in the fall?" Click the question to read the answer. In the topics area, kids can get help on specific topics like earthquakes or Martin Luther King, Jr.

The librarians don't give full answers, but their tips tell kids where to find the answers. The librarians always explain how they found the information on the Net and in the library. Kids should read that part of the answer so they can learn how to search the Web on their own.

If the FAQs don't answer every question, click the e-mail address at the bottom of the page for more help. Kids can send their questions to a librarian and get an answer back within two school days.

Answers to homework questions kids ask most

KidsConnect: Frequently Asked Questions

http://www.ala.org/ICONN/kcfaq.html

Kids have been doing homework for a long time. Therefore, a lot of the questions kids have probably aren't new. For instance, if someone wants to know about volcanoes, they can hit this hot site for all the info they need. This site already has answers to questions kids ask about these bubbling mountains. Look here for all the facts.

Links:

* ICONnect
* American Library Association

Online Activities

Kids can think of the Web as a giant library. It lets them look up information on almost any topic. But the Web is more exciting than a regular library. It brings thousands of hands-on activities right to a user's computer screen. Kids get a video game arcade, coloring book, storybook, card shop, and much more, all on their computers.

Some games that kids will find are fun action games like the ones they've played before. They might try to shoot a basketball through the hoop or sink the computer's aircraft carrier in a game of Battleship. But other Web games take children on new adventures. Cybersurfari and Headbone Derby give them the role of a detective, searching for clues all over the Internet. And that's a turf that just keeps expanding.

The most interesting online activities let kids try things they couldn't anywhere else. Ever send a musical birthday card to a friend? At the Blue Mountain Arts card shop, kids can send virtual cards that play cartoons and music through e-mail to friends and family. And best of all, these fun cards are free!

Bonus.com turns a kid's computer into an electronic playground. This colorful site, packed with games and cool graphics, really is a "SuperSite For Kids," just like it says.

The games are worth a visit all by themselves. Click the New Fun button on the main page and then click the Top 10 button to see the most popular games. Kids can test their skill at blasting spaceships in Starship Escape, or help girls hit the basket in Girls' Superdunk.

Users never know what will show up on their screen in the Imagine area. Sometimes, kids can try a news quiz to see how much they know about current events. Or they can look up great recipes. This section is always changing, just like people's imaginations!

The Explore section points kids to great lessons on all kinds of topics. They can read about things like why some people are left-handed, why Leonardo da Vinci was so important, or what's behind the meteorites buried beneath the ice in Antarctica.

There are also plenty of chances for kids to color pictures, get craft ideas, and read about animals. Bonus.com has so much to see that kids will keep coming back.

An online fun house packed with activities

BONUS.COM

http://www.bonus.com

Bonus.com has so many things to see that a few of its corners are bound to get a little "fishy." Explore the world under the ocean and meet some sharks. This is definitely one time kids will be glad that the Internet lets them "virtually" meet some creatures before they experience them in real life.

bonus.com

Kids don't just watch this channel, they get involved

THE KID'S CHANNEL

http://members.tripod.com/ ~ kid_channel/index.htm

Kids who love to make people laugh will have a ball with The Kid's Channel. They can send in their jokes and see how many people they make laugh. If kids know that the answer to "What goes up and down but doesn't move?" is "a staircase," they might be a big enough joker for this site.

Links:

* Kid's Cooking Corner
* KID STUFF
* Kids Korner

Kids will feel welcome right away at The Kid's Channel. When they type in their name, they'll see a personalized message. Then they can go on in and read a story, send postcards to friends, try recipes, or play games. Best of all, kids can help build the site by sending in their own creations.

Kid authors are ready to entertain users with stories and jokes at this site. Click the Stories button to read tales kids sent in such as "The Lost Dog" by 9-year-old Samantha. Jokes come straight from kids, too, and users can send in their own stories or jokes with the e-mail button. The Recipes section isn't just about food; it also tells kids how to make some neat crafts such as their own stickers. The Art Work section shows off pictures kids send in, and users can send in their own pictures to enter a monthly contest.

Try out a real antique video game in the Games area. Pong is like an electronic Ping-Pong game, and it's been around so long some kids' parents might have played it when they were young. Challenge them to a game and see who gets the better score.

Young kids can dig into an electronic toy box at the Enchanted Learning Software site. The activities here are just right for youngsters who are learning to read and beginning to discover everything around them.

The Little Explorers book link is a good place to start. This dictionary shows pictures of words starting with each letter of the alphabet. Click "K," for example, to see a kangaroo, kitten, keyboard, and more. Most of the words have links with more information on the object. This is a fun place to practice reading.

Neat stuff on the main page includes bird and dinosaur jokes, a connect-the-dots game, nursery rhymes, and flip books, where kids can mix parts of trucks and dinosaurs to make their own wild creations.

Zoom topics let kids check out places such as The Great Wall of China, Australia, Japan, and the United States. They can follow the links all over the pages to read whatever they think is most interesting. Zoom topics on countries teach users about the animals and history of the country, plus they will learn to make crafts from each country. Japan's craft is especially cool. It shows kids how to make animals out of folded paper.

Younger kids have fun while learning here

ENCHANTED LEARNING SOFTWARE

http://www.enchantedlearning.com/

It's easy to learn the alphabet when kids know a bunch of words that start with each letter. The Little Explorers book is a great reading tool that lets young kids see words that start with each letter. Click the links to learn more about everything from airplanes to zeppelins.

Links:
* Alive! Excellence In Education
* Jan's Kid Corner
* Cool Safe Links for Kids, Parents And Teachers

For a change, let the computer do the talking

READ-ALONG STORIES

http://www.indiana.edu/~eric_rec/fl/pcto/read.html

A friendly voice on the Internet can read kids a story before bedtime—or any other time—at this site. Kids can read the stories themselves, or click the speaker button to hear the story read out loud while they just look at the pictures and use their imaginations.

Links:

* Writer's Guidelines
* Parents And Children Online

Learning to read is a tough job, but the Read-along Stories site makes it a little easier. This online story-book has some cool tales to tell, plus a narrator's voice will read the story aloud with kids. That way they can follow along and hear someone else say any hard words they can't figure out. And if kids aren't in the mood to read, they can just listen to the narrator's voice. It's almost like having a real person read the story!

The site has a lot of different stories. In one tale, Emily explores the world with magic jelly beans. They help her travel to events such as baseball games and even places like Mexico. In another, Anne enters a forest to look for a scary monster called a Grindelstark. Another story tells about a boy who meets a bunch of angry cows. Fun pictures help kids follow along with each story.

Click the words at the top and bottom of the page for ideas of things to think about before and after reading each tale. At the end of the story about cows, for example, kids can think about why people should be kind to animals.

Coloring is fun, except when kids run out of pictures. Coloring books on the Internet don't have that problem. Users can color one picture 5 or 10 or 100 different ways on the screen to try out different looks. Most of them also let kids print out patterns so they can color on paper.

Kendra's Coloring Book is a good online coloring book to check out. It has plenty of pictures to color, and the site is easy to use for kids of all ages. Click Select A Picture To Color to see what kids can color. It might take a minute for the next page to appear. The user then can click the picture they want to color, such as the cow, frog, or silly robot. (Use the Print button to color the picture on paper.) Then click a color and click a part of the picture to color it. Kids don't color on this site by drawing lines. Instead, they are filling in parts of the picture with each color they choose. Click Clear to start over and color the picture again.

Kendra picks one picture for a contest each month and puts the winning picture on the site. Color it and click the Enter button to enter the contest.

Color pictures online or print pictures onto paper

KENDRA'S COLORING BOOK

http://www.geocities.com/ EnchantedForest/7155/

Kendra's Coloring Book gives kids plenty of colors to use in their drawings. However, if a user can't find just the right shade, Kendra lets kids create their own. Click Mix, then choose a couple of different colors to combine. Now kids will be drawing with their own, personal color!

Links:

* Scooby Doo's Coloring Book
* Draw And Color A Cartoony Party With Uncle Fred
* Carlos' Coloring Book

Kendra's Coloring Book

virtual gifts are waiting to be sent from this site

VIRTUAL FLOWERS AND GIFTS

http://www.en.com/users/felion/virtual.html

Want to make a friend's day better without spending a dime? Send them on vacation! The Virtual Gifts site lets kids send pictures of places like Hawaii or a mountain lake to anyone they want. When their friends get the message, they can forget their worries and think about the beautiful scenery.

It's the thought that counts. Here's a way to send cool presents without spending any money. The Virtual Flowers and Gifts site lets kids pick a great virtual present and send it through an e-mail message. Kids are really just sending a picture of something like flowers or a car, but they can pretend that it's real.

This site is perfect for making a friend's day with a fun message. If a pal really wants a sports car, get them one from this site. Kids might send one of these presents to Mom and Dad at work to let them know they're thinking about them.

This gift shop has presents for everybody on a child's list. Choose a bunch of online flowers and then type a special message like "Happy Birthday, Mom!" and send it in an e-mail message. Sometimes music can be added.

Flowers aren't for everybody, so look through the list for other gifts. Kids might want to send a virtual apple pie, virtual hugs and kisses, or an Awesome Award to somebody special.

For once, kids are the ones giving the quiz, not the ones taking it. In the Animal Guessing Game, the kids already know all the answers and the computer is the one trying to guess. The user's job is to think of an animal— any one they want. Then the computer asks the user questions as it tries to guess the animal that they see in their imagination.

Don't tell the computer what the animal is when visiting the site! Kids should just type in their name, so the computer knows who they are. Then the computer starts asking kids questions like "Can the animal fly?" or "Is it a very small animal?" Kids should make sure they know a lot about the animal they're thinking of. The computer asks some hard questions like "Does it like to chew bones?" When kids run out of animals to stump the computer, they can look around the Internet and learn about new animals. Then they can come back to this Web site and play again.

Sometimes the computer can't guess the animal in the kid's mind. Then they have to tell the computer a little about the animal so it can do a better job of guessing when the next kid thinks of that creature.

The computer tries to guess an animal in a kid's imagination

ANIMAL GUESSING GAME

http://www.bushnet.qld.edu.au/animal

Users should try to imagine the weirdest animal they can. Then, visit this site to see if the computer can guess the one they're thinking of. Try something like an aardvark. The computer will take a long time to guess this one by asking questions like "Does it have horns?" and "Can you ride it?"

Links:

* BushNet Home Page
* BushScene
* Earth Science Australia

Find e-mail pen pals from around the world

KEYPALS CLUB INTERNATIONAL

http://www.worldkids.net/clubs/kci/

When kids make electronic pen pals from around the world in Keypals Club International, the world comes alive at their fingertips. One member says the club might even stop wars in the future. Maybe if kids everywhere got worldwide exposure and learned how to get along now, they'll be better prepared when they grow up and start running their countries.

Ever talked to someone from Croatia? Kids can on the Internet. The Net is one of the greatest places invented for meeting people kids would never get to otherwise. And one of the greatest places to meet people on the Net is the Keypals Club International, the site designed to help kids ages 8 to 16 get in touch with more than 11,400 other members around the globe. It's even built by a 12-year-old named Lauren.

When kids join the Keypals Club, they'll start exchanging e-mail and other electronic messages with kids from places such as Trinidad, Croatia, and Singapore. Users will get as many pen pals as they want immediately! Members share notes about their lives, plus scary Creepy Corner stories, jokes, recipes, and help with homework. When kids are thinking about joining, they should visit the Web site and check out the FAQs for the scoop on what the club's all about and how they can join.

Kids curious about what's going on outside their neighborhood should get involved in this site. They'll learn about new ways of life from the people actually living them—a great way to make the things that kids read in textbooks come alive.

Lots of kids build clubhouses or tree houses where they can hang out with their friends and play games. KidsCom is like one of those clubhouses on the Internet. It's a perfect place for kids from all over to hang out, make friends, and have a great time. Anyone can join for free.

Click Make New Friends to meet other cool kids. Kids can sign up for a key pal (a pen pal who kids talk to through e-mail) who is interested in the same things they are. Go into the Graffiti Wall chat area to have live, typed "conversations" on the screen. The adults working for KidsCom make sure that no bad guys get into the Graffiti Wall.

KidsCom helps make sure adults—really important ones—listen to what the kids have to say. The Voice To The World section lets a kid send a message about things like the environment and world hunger straight to the people running whole countries, including the United States. Users can tell other kids what they think by clicking the Kids Talk About section and posting messages about poll topics or even their pet.

Then, kids can cut loose with some online video games or stretch their imaginations by writing stories they can send in.

The ultimate electronic clubhouse for kids

KidsCom

http://www.kidscom.com/

Kids' opinions count at KidsCom. Every week a new poll lets members say what they think about such issues as "How old should a person be before they are allowed to get a driver's license?" Kids send in their thoughts, and then they can read about what other kids think about these issues.

KidsCom

Adopt a pretend pet and take good care of it

VIRTUAL PUPPY

http://www.virtualpuppy.com

Kids can visit their puppy online every day to make sure it's healthy and happy. When one score gets low, it means the dog's getting hungry. Click the Food button to fill up its dish (and stomach). When it looks unhappy, throw a Frisbee for it and have some fun.

Links:

* Virtual Kitty
* Mail-A-Pup

Keep a pet inside the computer. This isn't some new kind of crazy insect that can survive on electronic signals. They're computer programs kids care for, just like a real pet. The virtual puppies and kitties are like the digital toys that kids all over have been taking care of. The puppies and kitties don't have all of the animation of real pets, but caring for them is fun.

Kids can adopt and name a puppy or kitty for free. Then they must visit their pet online to make sure it's happy, well fed, healthy, and clean. If the number score for any area gets too low, the caretaker needs to do something. They can click a few buttons to feed their pet, clean up after it, or even play with it. When kids aren't with the pet, it can sleep. If the pet owner forgets to take care of their animal, it could be bad news for their new pet!

If kids are thinking about getting a real pet, try adopting a virtual puppy or kitty first. These electronic animals aren't quite like the real thing, but if a kid can take care of one of these pets, they might be ready for a real one.

Good detectives needed! If kids think they can solve a mystery with clues spread around the world, then they may be ready to go on a Cybersurfari. This online treasure hunt sends kids on a mission to find information spread around the Web. Pay attention to the clues and have your Web skills ready.

The official contest ran during the fall of 1998, but a new season's around the corner, and the practice questions on the home page will keep young cyber-sleuths busy. Play alone or get some classmates together to make a team.

Here's how it works. Kids will read clues listing the treasure that they are after and where to find it. Follow the links to the sites that have the information hiding somewhere inside. Dig up the right information and get a secret treasure code. Whoever finds the most treasure codes wins. Questions might point kids to a space exploration page so they can find out how much a space shuttle carries. Or clues might lead kids to find out what vegetable was carved as the first jack-o'-lantern.

Be careful! Young detectives might get so interested in sites they're visiting that they forget all about the Cybersurfari!

Cyber-sleuths scour the Web for clues in this detective game

CYBERSURFARI '98

http://www.spa.org/cybersurfari/default.htm

A kid's first case as a Cybersurfari detective might be to follow the clues to find a large carnivore that lives in a swamp. These animals are usually brown, but this guy's white. Follow the links to the Audubon site and look for that white alligator and his treasure code.

Links:

* Excited Players!
* How To Play

An online arcade that makes learning fun

JumpStart Kids Game Center

http://www.kidspace.com/kids/games/

Does throwing darts at the bull's-eye sound like math homework? Does shooting cannon balls sound like studying? Maybe not, but both games really help kids learn at the JumpStart Kids Game Center site. When kids learn the right angles, every cannon shot will be right on target.

Links:

* Knowledge Adventure
* 3-D Dinosaur Adventure

If kids get bored with the video games they have, go online. This site collects a bunch of games in an arcade where kids can play for free. Be ready to think while you play. These games help kids practice their math and reading skills while they're having fun. (Don't worry; this is more fun than any homework.)

Choose a game from the main page and wait for it to load. While waiting, read the instructions on the left side of the screen. The games are simple enough that every kid should find a couple to play. Gamers don't need quick hands to play the basic games. A tile game has kids slide parts of a picture around until the picture comes together. Another good game for younger kids puts them to work solving simple math problems to connect dots.

Get ready for quick thinking in games such as the Frog Well, where kids shoot a frog's tongue at the numbers needed to complete math problems. The Lemonade Stand game shows kids how hard it can be to run a business. Kids decide how much lemonade to make each day and what to charge for each cup. Watch the weather forecast! Cloudy days slow down the sales.

The race is on, and the slowest kid in school or the smallest person in class could beat everyone else in the Headbone Derby. The winner is whoever's best at digging up facts on the Internet. In the Internet Research Adventures, kids help comic strip characters Iz and Auggie gather information to solve their cases. Read the comics to follow the heroes' story, then jump in when they need some information.

Assignments take Iz and Auggie around the earth and into outer space. Players might be looking for secrets of solar power in one episode and the names of musical composers or Martian canyons in another. Kids need to figure out where to look for the important information.

Sign up for a free Headbone Zone membership alone or as a team to join the derbies. As kids gather each piece of information from the Internet (or anywhere else they can find it), they'll earn points that can help them win great prizes such as software and toys. When kids get stumped, they can always ask for a hint. But getting hints takes points off a team's score—as does sending in a wrong answer. Kids should make sure they have the right facts before sending in their guesses.

Join the race to find facts online

HEADBONE DERBY

http://www.headbone.com/derby/

Iz and Auggie need help! They're stranded on Mars, and all their computer files were destroyed. To figure out what's going on, they need to know the name of a comet that was discovered on the same day by two different people. Join the Headbone Derby and start looking for the information. They're waiting!

Links:

* Prizes
* Headbone Zone
* Ecology Strikes Back!

Fun electronic cards make any occasion special

BLUE MOUNTAIN ARTS

http://www.bluemountain.com/

When a teacher does something really nice, kids can let them know that they appreciate it. Send an e-mail card that gives them the "Special Teacher Award." When they open the card, they'll hear a happy song that will really make them feel special.

Links:

* Blue Mountain Poetry Contest
* Card Pickup Window

It's fun getting birthday cards, but don't they all pretty much look the same? What if kids could get a card that plays music and shows their name in big, dancing letters? It's all possible at the Blue Mountain Arts site, which lets anybody send great electronic cards for a birthday, graduation, vacation, or any other special event for free.

Lots of Web sites let you send digital postcards with a picture and a message you type. But this site's cards are more fun because they add cartoons and sounds. Send friends an e-mail message saying that they have a card at the Blue Mountain site. When they open the card, they can see a greeting such as the one with jumping frogs that play a birthday song. Kids can show their parents how great they think they are by sending them a musical Best-Ever-Dad or Amazing Mom certificate.

This card shop has greetings for almost any occasion, including saying thank you, welcoming someone back from a trip, or even for regular holidays. Special sections offer cards with themes like wolves and Girl Scouts. These musical cards are a great way to show someone you're thinking of them; plus it's fun for kids to pick them.

When it's time for a story, kids don't always have to grab a book off the shelf. Visit Children's Storybooks Online. This little electronic library is full of all kinds of great tales about animals, adventures, and even the alphabet. There are stories for kids of all ages. Little readers can learn about things such as the sounds farm animals make, and older kids can check out adventures such as the story of Sliver Pete, the Old West cowpoke. Kids will find stories here about ponds, fairy tales, animals, and even strange creatures called wumpalumps.

Every story has great pictures. Some even move around, so kids should make sure they keep their eyes open for jumping gorillas and planes flying loop-de-loops. A few sound effects even pop up here and there.

Be sure to read the story about Buzzy Bee, the site's most popular character. The bottom of the main page features a couple of Buzzy Bee riddles and a maze game. Pictures from the Buzzy story are in the Buzzy Bee Coloring Book, so kids can print the pictures and color them.

And if kids are just looking for some regular paper books to read, click the Book Reviews button for recommendations on great books for kids.

Stories on the computer can really come alive

CHILDREN'S STORYBOOKS ONLINE

http://www.magickeys.com/ books/index.html

Some online picture books are way better than the ones printed on paper. This site's story about "Animals You Can See At The Zoo" has drawings of animals that really move. If kids listen closely, they can even hear an occasional lion's roar or an elephant's trumpet.

Links:

* Kid's Mall
* The Littlest Knight
* Candlelight Stories

The Elephant Book

Play with wild animals in these games

SEDGWICK COUNTY ZOO FUN STUFF

http://www.scz.org/fun/right.html

Animals at this zoo hide in some pretty weird places. In the Word Scramble, animals are hiding by mixing up the letters in their names. Kids will get so excited that they might roar when they figure out the animal's name that's mixed up in the letters "nilo."

Those eyes staring out at kids from the computer screen sure look familiar. But it's hard to tell what kids are seeing because the rest of the picture is missing! It would probably be best to print out this Web page, grab a pencil, and start connecting the dots to see the owner of those eyes. Kids can be sure it's one of the residents of the Sedgwick County Zoo (in Wichita, Kansas). All the games, puzzles, quizzes, and other activities at this Web page deal with the animals living at the zoo.

The games send kids on safaris to find animals hiding in puzzles. Print each page and start hunting. In the Herpetarium Seek and Find, kids will search for the names of animals that might live in the amphibian and reptile house. In Follow the Maze, help a baby bird find its nest by drawing a line through the maze in the tree. Watch out for the snakes! Most of these games are even fun for little kids.

Test your animal IQ with quizzes. Who Am I? is an animal guessing game. Kids get a clue about an animal like, "I am considered to be the king of the beasts" and then have to guess the animal's name. Check the answers with the boxes below each question.

When kids need an online expert to show them what's fun on the Web, they should go see Bonnie. She uses her site to point out the best (and most fun) kid activities around. There are enough cool ideas to keep kids busy surfing the Web for weeks. Bonnie helps kids find stories to read, recipes to try, and things to do when they're not using the PC. Some of her best pointers suggest games to play all over the Web. Kids click Play A Game and will then choose Play An Easy Game or Play A Harder Game to get activities that match their skill level. Everybody will be able to find a game right for them.

The Easy Games are perfect for younger kids. Try Franklin Dress-Up to put funny clothes on Franklin the turtle. Play Tic-Tac-Toe with Mario from the Nintendo games. He gives kids the "X," so they get to make the first move!

Bonnie shows kids where to give their brains a tougher workout in the section of harder games. Some are online versions of games kids might already play, such as Battleship. Kids can try to sink the computer's battleship before it sinks theirs. Or try a game of Hangman and guess the secret word before the stick man runs out of time.

BONNIE'S FUN THINGS

http://www2.arkansas.net/ ~mom/bonnie.html

Bonnie knows where to find all kinds of games, not just high-speed action games. For example, try What In The Universe? (Also called "Who Would've Guessed It?") This photo game shows kids a picture from an unusual angle. Things sure look different in these pictures. It is the user's job to guess what familiar object they are seeing in a new way.

Links:

* Send A Card
* Sing A Song
* Holiday Fun

Explore the World

The jungle rains are dripping on big, green leaves. There's a lion roaring just over the next hill. The smoke's so thick from the volcano belching fire over the treetops that the giant iceberg sliding closer almost sneaks by!

Icebergs in a jungle? The only way to visit a place this wild is through a computer. The Web sites in Explore the World provide the ticket to every part of the earth after just a few minutes of Web surfing. Sultry rain forests and floating icebergs sit on pages right next to each other. Audio and video clips make it seem like kids really have stepped into exotic locations.

Of course, there is a lot more to see in the world than just nature. The Web provides tours of famous museums such as The Smithsonian Institution and landmarks like The White House. Other expeditions include visits to people living in other countries across the oceans. Spending some time in other countries teaches kids that people may do things differently, but also that all humans have a lot in common!

The animals are all ready for a visit, so there's no reason to wait. Kids can drop by the St. Louis Zoo site to try out lots of neat activities and gather information. The St. Louis Zoo's Web site is a good one to explore, but it can also show what's available in zoo sites in general.

A lot of the information at this site comes in handy when planning a real visit to the St. Louis Zoo. But all the online animal information provides a zoo visit even for kids who never go to St. Louis. Visitors click the Animals button to see a zoo map, then click an area to visit. There are photos of each animal and information to read about how they live.

Links on the main page provide visitors with special zoo news. In the springtime, there usually are stories about new animal babies. The Kids link is the shortcut to info made just for young people. Fun activities include animal picture puzzles and coloring pages. There's also a chance to read up on the animals that might be living in everyone's backyard and what kids can do to help them. Stories go behind the scenes to teach about things like how zookeepers spend their days.

Visit wild animals at the zoo without leaving the room

ST. LOUIS ZOO

http://www.stlzoo.org/home.asp

It's easy to be a real part of a zoo by adopting an animal for $25 with parents' help. Animal adopters get a certificate, photo of the animal, T-shirt, and facts about the animal. The animals, such as a giraffe, chimp, or Asian elephant, stay at the zoo, but the adopters now help them live!

Links:

* Learning
* Conservation/Research
* Group Fun

Frankly one of the best museums on the Web

THE FRANKLIN INSTITUTE SCIENCE MUSEUM

http://sln.fi.edu/

Benjamin Franklin did a lot more than fly a kite in a thunderstorm. He was one of the smartest men who ever lived in the United States. A stroll through the exhibit about his life shows his inventions, all the different jobs he tried, and even a game where kids can learn about how electricity works.

Links:

* Educational Hotlists
* Favorite Online Schools
* Powers Of Nature

Visiting the Franklin Institute Science Museum's Web site is almost as good as visiting a museum in person. The awesome exhibits here cover every area of science from earthquakes to living things to old Ben Franklin himself. The best part is, this museum is open whenever kids want to visit.

The EARTHFORCE link offers "moving" lessons on how the earth constantly shakes, rattles, and rolls because of forces like earthquakes, volcanoes, and tidal waves. Articles tell all about what would happen if people could dig a hole all the way to the center of the earth. They'd find burning rock, and this exhibit tells how that hot rock moves around to create volcanoes. Links on every topic help users explore the information as much as they want.

The online exhibit about a human heart is especially interesting. It pays to know all about this special muscle pump that keeps people alive. A special report explains the heart's job.

Biopoint is a free pass to drop in on a real science class as it tackles projects like dissecting a crayfish (that's like a tiny lobster). The pictures help kids follow along just as if they're in the lab.

Everybody's neighborhood is a little different, but for kids living in places like the Amazon rain forest or Africa, life is very different. Visitors can hang out with some of these kids for a while at the Let's Go!: Around the World site to see how their lives are different from those of American kids.

Clicking the frog starts a visit to the rain forest; clicking the elephant whisks kids away to Africa. Tours of the Amazon come through the eyes of the kids that live there. Visitors see the amazing things that are part of this area's residents' everyday world, just like the school bus is part of the world for kids in America. The pictures of these kids show what their lives are like. Does their skin or hair look different than kids' here? How about their clothes? Flipping through these pictures is like looking at a photo album from a faraway country.

Click the Tell Me About It! icon to learn about pictures on the site. Kids can learn that the biggest girl in one picture has to look after her little sisters while she tries to play, too. Does that sound familiar to American kids?

Take a break for a little fun with games like those in the Safari! section of the African tour. Mystery animals write poems that help kids guess their identities.

Tour foreign lands with the kids who live there

LET'S GO!: AROUND THE WORLD

http://www.ccph.com/

African kids working on their math don't add four and seven to come up with 11. They add "nne" and "saba." Anybody can add like that, too, after taking some Swahili language lessons at the Let's Go! site. Students learn enough words here to make one million Swahili sentences!

AMERICAN MUSEUM OF NATURAL HISTORY

http://www.amnh.org/

Join museum scientists on big expe-ditions to places such as the Gobi desert, the bottom of the ocean, and even the planet Mars. Follow the pictures and stories to explore the wildest places in the universe. Visitors try out what they've seen with challenges like reading an ocean map.

Links:

* Young Naturalist Awards
* Research
* Imax Films

When it comes to history, people usually think about things people have done. Most history classes cover important topics like wars, kings, and scientists. But the American Museum of Natural History shows that there's a lot more to history than just people. Studying natural history is all about learning the earth's life story. This museum in New York City is a fun place to do it.

Anyone living near the museum can use the site to learn about its exhibits and plan a visit. Even for kids far from the museum, though, this Web site has plenty to see. The Explore section describes nature activities for kids ages 4 to 7 to do with their parents. Kids work just like real scientists in projects such as building a diorama (that's like a model) of a wading bird rookery or rain forest. Users test their observation skills by describing the differences between types of leaves.

The Electronic Newspaper has exciting articles about topics such as how museum workers put together dinosaur skeletons. The Sci-Q Quiz (in the Education section) tests kids' knowledge with questions about topics like the highest mountain on Earth and what kinds of living things are most numerous on the planet. (Hint: It's not people!)

Disneyland is known as "the happiest place on Earth." It got its name from a marketing slogan, but kids and adults alike can't help but have fun at this giant amusement park. The Disneyland Web site offers a fun tour of what's at the real Disneyland. Anyone planning to visit Disneyland can use this site to figure out what to see when they arrive. And even folks who can't make it to Disneyland can take a pretend tour online.

Explore Disneyland has highlights of all the major park areas, such as Frontierland, Fantasyland, and Critter Country. Visitors learn about the rides and attractions, shops, and places to eat in each area. Some of the best parts of this section are exciting rides such as the Matterhorn Bobsleds.

The Business and Education section lists special events that take place at Disneyland each year. Also check out the Art Lessons section. Kids might be able to talk their parents or teachers into doing some of the cool lessons available for downloading.

Take a make-believe trip to a fantasy theme park

DISNEYLAND

http://www2.disney.com/Disneyland/index.html?GL=H

Here's how to visit the home of the world's most famous mouse. Mickey's Toontown at Disneyland lets kids stroll through the homes of favorite Disney characters such as Mickey Mouse and Chip 'n Dale. Read all about this wonderful neighborhood at the Disneyland site.

Links:

* Magic Music Days
* Family.com

Get up close and personal with dinosaurs

DINOSAUR INFORMATION SHEETS

http://www.childrensmuseum.org/dino.htm

Dinosaur facts never get boring! Tyrannosaurus Rex sure looks like a scary giant in the movies. But this ferocious dinosaur was really pretty puny compared to the biggest dinosaurs. T. Rex weighed about six tons, but the Brachiosaurus weighed in at about 55 tons. That's as much as 11 elephants!

The pages in this Web site are like baseball cards for the scariest animals that ever lived. The Dinosaur Information Sheets provide pictures of dinosaurs and throw in all the facts about each animal. This site from The Children's Museum of Indianapolis is the perfect place to start any dinosaur research for school or just for fun.

Kids look through the list of dinosaur names and click an animal such as Tyrannosaurus Rex. They'll see a color picture of the dinosaur pop up on the screen. All those teeth, claws, and horns add up to something nobody would want to mess with! Under the picture are all the facts about the dinosaur. Read about what T. Rex and his dino buddies ate and how big they were. T. Rex's teeth were each six inches long. Visitors should measure six inches on a ruler to get a better idea of the size of these monstrous creatures. Kids can click a link to print out a picture they can then color. Anyone who colors enough pictures can start their own dinosaur hall of fame.

The FAQs (frequently asked questions) about dinosaurs answer common questions such as "What is the largest known dinosaur?" and "How do dinosaurs get their names?"

Wild America can be tough and strong, but the animals and land still need help from kids. That's why the National Wildlife Federation built this kids' Web site. Kids should stop here to learn what's best for wild animals and their environments. Visitors turn into real junior wildlife experts.

Cool Tours are a good way to start wildlife training. Journey through wetlands and public lands and learn about important topics such as endangered species and the water cycle. There are even cool experiments to try, such as creating a water cycle at home. Kids can make a system that runs just like the rain and lakes in the real world. The tour ends when kids answer quiz questions about what they just learned.

Lots of young wildlife fans read *Ranger Rick* magazine. Now they can read several of the magazine's articles online. Rick's Homework section highlights Web sites that help kids with assignments.

On-line Games let kids match animal tracks with names such as coyote, muskrat, and chicken. The More Fun! button covers cool things to do outside. Kids can be their own meteorologist by building a rain gauge, or hunt for different plants and animals around town.

Fun facts and activities about wildlife and the environment

NATIONAL WILDLIFE FEDERATION FOR KIDS

http://www.nwf.org/kids/

Even kids living in a big city can get to know the environment better by attracting animals to their backyards. This site offers ideas such as building a snowman with a necklace made of bird seed. Keep notes on what kinds of birds show up to eat the necklace.

Links:

* National Wildlife Federation
* Take Action!

A kids' guide to animals on the Web

ZooNet for Kids

http://members.aol.com/zoonetkids/index.htm

Almost everybody knows what a killer whale looks like. But it's a little harder to tell a dorsal fin from a pectoral flipper. The Whale-Times link on the ZooNet page quizzes kids about these and other whale facts. Plus, visitors can read about those killer whales—they can live to be 35 years old!

Links:

* Rhinos And Tigers And Bears—Oh My!
* WhaleTimes
* Trek Kids
* Zoo Camp

To see animals in real life, people go to the jungle or the zoo. To see animals on the Web, people should go to ZooNet for Kids. This site gets kids started on a safari around the Internet to see any kind of animal they can imagine.

The link sections help everyone find the animal info they need. Choose from pages for real-life children's zoos (maybe the local zoo is here), educational sites, zoo sites just for kids, and animal pictures and sounds. Anyone can create their own animal adventure by following different links.

The Cub Den is one of the great sites available through ZooNet. The Den is all about bears and people who want to know more about them. It's packed with amazing facts about bears. Everyone knows that koala bears are cute. But who knew that they're not really bears at all? They're more like kangaroos!

The Kids' Page from Micke Grove Zoo talks about being a zookeeper. These folks have learned to build cages that look like the places where wild animals live. That way animals are happier, and visitors get to see them acting as they would in their natural homes.

What can kids find when they dig through an old trunk full of stuff in grandma's attic? There are probably all kinds of old-fashioned treasures. Imagine digging through the attic of our whole country! That's like visiting The Smithsonian Institution. This group of museums in Washington, D.C., collects everything from dinosaur bones to the first airplane.

Visitors should start by clicking Resources & Tours, then go to the bottom of the page and choose "A Kid's Guide to the Smithsonian." This tour covers the National Museum of American History, the National Air & Space Museum, and the National Museum of Natural History. Each museum has links to some of its most popular exhibits. In the American History museum, kids can see the flag that inspired America's national anthem.

Pictures of many items in the museum are on the Web site. A search tool lets kids jump right to the pictures they would like to see. It's easy to look up photos of the first spaceship used to visit the moon or of favorite dinosaurs. Other tools, such as the Encyclopedia Smithsonian, help users look up facts on almost any topic.

THE SMITHSONIAN INSTITUTION HOME PAGE

http://www.si.edu/newstart.htm

Most people don't save all their old clothes, but The Smithsonian Institution museum holds on to a lot of old clothes. Visitors can even see a uniform worn by George Washington, America's first president. Check out a picture of these famous clothes at the museum's Web site.

Links:

* The History Of The Smithsonian
* Art, Design, and Crafts
* Smithsonian On-Line Catalogue
* National Postal Museum

Computers teach about computer history on
a kid's computer

THE COMPUTER MUSEUM NETWORK

http://www.tcm.org/html/galleries/ network/index.html

When computers start talking to each other, they can do amazing jobs. The Web is a great example of what's possible when computers share information. The Networks Gallery at The Computer Museum Network points out networks that affect life every day in areas such as medicine and mail.

Links:

* Kids & Computer:
* Careers in Comp
* Computer Clubho

Computers have sure changed since they were invented. Some of the first computers filled a whole room! A visit to The Computer Museum Network teaches interesting facts, such as how computers have gotten smaller as they've gotten more powerful. This site can help older kids learn about computers for school or just for fun.

The History button provides a quick computer history lesson. Every day, visitors learn a fact about a different computer event. The computer time line lists major events for each year. Kids will have to do their studying at some other sites too, though. This time line only goes up to 1990. That's ancient history in the computer world.

Real computer nuts should visit the Galleries for a detailed study of topics such as Networks and Robots. These sections explain how computers around the world work together and how machines can do some of our work for us. A cool network game lets kids work with friends on the Internet to put a picture together. It really shows what everyone can do with the right network. Many of the words in the articles can be clicked to reach more information, so users can study each topic as much as they want.

The home of the president of the United States is no ordinary house, and the pet cat living in the White House is no ordinary feline. Socks, President Clinton's cat, makes a great tour guide as he takes kids on a trip through our country's most famous house. This cat shares all the facts about the history and construction of the White House. For instance, kids will learn that Washington, D.C., started as a big swamp with pigs roaming the streets. Kids see lots of pictures and learn about some adventurous moments in the White House halls, such as the time Dolley Madison rescued a painting of George Washington from a raging fire.

Socks' tour gives kids a feel for what it's like to be a president's kid living in the White House. It's definitely not all business. Some of the jokes Abraham Lincoln's son Tad used to play are really crazy! Of course Socks is fond of animals, so he shares some pictures of White House pets such as Caroline Kennedy's pony Macaroni. Visitors see that animals play a big part in our nation's number one home, making Socks the "purrfect" insider to show kids around.

Tour the president's house with his pet cat

THE WHITE HOUSE FOR KIDS

http://www.whitehouse.gov/WH/kids/html/home.html

The President's cat, Socks, provides inside access on this White House tour. Guests even get a chance to send e-mail from this Web page to the president or vice president. Kids who include their addresses will get a reply in the mail!

Links:

* White House Kids
* White House Pets
* White House Home Page

Join earth's greatest adventurers from the safety of home

NATIONALGEOGRAPHIC. COM/KIDS

http://www.nationalgeographic. com/kids

Get up close and personal with Myrtle the turtle, a 400-pound green sea turtle, at the National Geographic site. Workers at the New England Aquarium in Boston placed a tiny "Crittercam," a small video camera, on her back to see if it affected her behavior. The study concluded that it did not cause any difference in her behavior, and now studies like this are going on all over the world.

Links:

* National Geographic Television
* Geography Resources
* Cartoon Factory

The world is pretty big, but the National Geographic Society has seen most of it. These adventurers travel the planet to check out amazing people, places, and animals. Anyone can see what they've been doing at National Geographic's online area for kids.

The Amazing Travel Bureau takes visitors on exciting adventures with people such as scientists who walk on volcanoes to gather information. Try the extras like animations showing how the earth works. Read some amazing stories from *World* magazine for kids. There's even a story from one woman who rode on the *Titanic* when she was 12 (and survived!). Kids who have something to say on any topic can get on the Kids Network to post their opinions for everyone else to read.

Have some fun with knowledge in the Fun & Games area. Kids can laugh at the jokes and tongue twisters or test their brains with the Geo Bee Challenge. These are real questions from the National Geography Bee.

Older kids should be sure to visit Xpeditions. The area shows printable maps of almost any place on earth. It's great for school projects. A walk through the Xpedition Hall lets visitors run amazing machines like the one that demonstrates ecosystems.

Kids in places such as Australia and Israel live far from here, so they probably live a lot differently than Americans. Kids can find out for sure on a Culture Quest where they try out life in other countries. Olivia Owl and Parsifal Penguin are ready to explain how all kinds of different people live.

This trip with Olivia and Parsifal is a lot better than a plain book about other countries. These two birds show users what other countries are really like. For example, there are stories other kids hear before they go to bed. Greek kids hear the story about a wolf in sheep's clothing, just like the one lots of American kids are familiar with.

Kids in Israel eat foods such as avocado with honey, and this recipe (plus a lot more) is right on the site. Kids could surprise their class by bringing a foreign food to school the next time they have to take treats. New games let users pretend they're a kid in Brazil or another country. Brazilian kids love playing Sick Cat. Will kids in American neighborhoods like it?

Culture Quest is a big help for social studies classes, but it also shows that American kids aren't the only ones with some great ideas for having a good time.

Broaden horizons by crossing virtual, cultural boundaries

CULTURE QUEST

http://www.ipl.org/youth/cquest/

Here's a place to spend the day living like kids in another country. Culture Quest takes visitors to places such as Japan, where kids learn to say "konnichiwa" instead of "hello." Japanese recipes let users make a lunch of miso soup for the family, then try a game of Japanese tag.

Links:

* Internet Public Library Youth Page
* Resources on countries visited

Real-life adventures from around the globe

THE DISCOVERY CHANNEL ONLINE

http://www.discovery.com/online.html

Don't throw away that rock! It might be a bone from an old dinosaur. Scientists have to look carefully at everything in the ground when digging for bones in the Gobi desert. Everyone can find out what else scientists on this job worry about by joining this Discovery Channel expedition.

Links:

* Africa's Elephant Kingdom
* Discovery Channel School
* The Learning Channel
* Animal Planet

The best stories are about the real world people live in. Everything from the oceans to the sky to the human body holds exciting adventures. The Discovery Channel Online is a personal ticket to worlds most people have never seen.

A visit to the Feature Stories and Expeditions produces people such as a businessman who's chasing the world's biggest floating ice cubes. He's capturing icebergs and melting them down to sell as drinking water! A special section answers questions everybody wonders about such as "Why is snow white?"

Sometimes it seems like this Web site is actually part of the Discovery Channel on television. Pictures, videos, and audio clips make most of the stories come alive, so visitors won't just read about bear cubs, they'll hear them calling for their mom! The Animal Cams show pictures taken just one minute earlier of famous animals such as panda bears and Keiko the killer whale.

Kids share their opinions on topics in the Conversations area. Or, build your brain by taking a quiz in identifying famous people in history. Everyone should enjoy something at this site, but good readers should get the most from the stories.

ideas for Real Life

There is a lot of information on the Web that can help kids have more fun or get great ideas for what they do every day. Kids can visit this section's sites, then turn off the computer and use their new ideas in real life.

Some of the ideas help people live longer and better. Try out sites such as Safety City and 10 Tips to Healthy Eating & Physical Activity. Vince & Larry, the crash test dummies at Safety City, teach kids why they should wear seat belts. The 10 Tips site help kids eat healthy food that includes vegetables as well as their favorite stuff such as pizza and ice cream.

Children will find instructions for some real hands-on projects hidden in a lot of these sites. Kids can get plans for folding the world's greatest paper airplanes. Or they can start a career as a magician by learning simple magic tricks with objects around the house. Kids can show their artistic skills with a few craft projects. All kinds of hints and tips exist on the Web to help make kids' time away from the computer more fun and interesting.

SUMMER FUN

http://www.netfix.com/poptart/summer.htm

There's a mystery in every kid's mouth when they play Summer Fun's Taste Testing game. Put on a blindfold and have some friends put different foods in a bag. Grab something out of the bag, take a bite, and try to guess what it is!

Sometimes kids forget that summer's a time for having fun, not getting bored. It's no fun just sitting around and watching television. The Summer Fun site can help get kids going with tons of great activity ideas. Some of the suggestions are for simple games to keep kids busy, but others describe awesome projects they can try.

Kids can get their hands dirty with a little gardening, for instance. The Garden Fun section tells kids how to grow all kinds of plants of their very own. Young gardeners can start a little farm with lima bean sprouts, sweet potato vines, and carrots. Kids will even find instructions here for growing a house out of bean stalks!

The recipes help kids whip up some cool summer treats. It only takes graham crackers, bananas, and whipped cream to make delicious banana cream pies that kids can chomp in a few bites. Or try making some homemade Popsicles.

When the weather turns nasty, check out the ideas in the Summer Fun's Indoor Fun section. Kids can ignore the bad weather with inside activities such as making watercolors from scratch and then letting their imaginations go with an afternoon of painting.

Kids can open up their own restaurant for birds if they keep drinking their milk. Just finish off the milk in the fridge, then grab that cardboard milk carton before Mom and Dad recycle it. (A cardboard juice carton will work just as well.) Now kids have all they need to start their own deluxe bird diner in the backyard. When kids finish this project, they will get to see lots of lively birds hanging around their home.

This site is a great example of the wildlife projects kids can learn on the Web. A diagram made by real wildlife experts shows kids how to turn an old carton into a perfect bird feeder. It only takes a few cuts here and there. Then make a hanger. Next, follow the suggested recipes for birds' favorite meals. The best mixes include suet, millet, and maybe even dog biscuits. You'll find everything you need at the pet or grocery store.

Once kids read up on where to place their feeder (make sure squirrels can't raid the feeder), they begin the waiting game (especially in winter). Sometimes it takes a while for the birds to find the food people have left them. After a while, though, the birds will remember where the feeder is, and the child will become an important part of their world.

This site isn't just for the birds!

MILK CARTON BIRD FEEDER

http://www.dfw.state.or.us/ODFWhtml/Education/BirdFeeder.html

Bird watching can really take flight when kids place a bird feeder outside their window. Follow the diagram to build a feeder and keep it stocked with seed (or whatever the child decides to use). In the winter, birds learn to rely on meals people give them, and kids learn about responsibility. Kids then become an important part of the wildlife community!

Write songs and make music with everyday objects

PIPSQUEAKS

http://www.childrensmusic.org/ Pipsqueaks.html

There's a songwriter in every kid waiting to come out. Pipsqueaks gives kids a chance to show that talent by writing new verses for an old song called "Cindy." Add your own words to this tune about yucky girls. Pipsqueaks also wants girls to send in their own words about gross boys.

Links:

* Children's Music Web
* Kids' Radio
* Hand Jive

Music is a big part of real life. A good tune helps everybody from adults to little kids get through the day with a smile. Imagine how boring the radio or movies would be without any music! That's never a problem at the Pipsqueaks site. Its musical goodies will keep kids' toes tapping wherever they go.

The main idea at Pipsqueaks is to have fun with music. Try singing along with real audio clips of silly songs written by other kids. Some first graders wrote a funny song about Elvis the butterfly. Kids can listen to it and see what they think. Then jump over to the Tall and Small Reviews to see what kids and adults think of the same music albums.

Kids can play radio star by recording their own radio program. Pipsqueaks tells kids how to set up a recording studio in their closet and how to make cool sound effects for the show.

The great thing about music is that anybody can play it, even if they can't play an instrument like the piano or guitar. The Create section shows kids that anything can be an instrument, even spoons or their own heartbeats. Artis the Spoonman and other musicians give kids lessons in playing common objects such as teaspoons.

Vince and Larry know a lot about being unsafe. In fact, their whole job is to have bad accidents every day. But these crash test dummies kids have seen on TV commercials are glad to do it. Vince and Larry learn safety tips that they can then pass on to kids. Learn from all their wrecks by reading their safety advice on the Web.

The crash dummies are famous for their car wrecks and seat belt safety, but they can teach kids to be safe in a lot of different places. Kids can click Safety School to start their lessons on avoiding injuries. The Safety Challenge tests how much kids know—and shows what they need to study.

The Bike Tour button teaches pedal-pushers really important biking tips. Vince and Larry help kids learn: how to check their bike equipment; how to ride correctly around cars; and how to watch out for Danger Zones around town.

Vince and Larry have been in over 10,000 crashes in the Research Lab. Read about what happens to people in car crashes and how seat belts can save lives. Then kids will see why only real dummies don't buckle up.

Learn safety smarts from a pair of famous dummies

SAFETY CITY

http://www.nhtsa.dot.gov/kids/

We call Vince and Larry crash test "dummies," but they're smart when it comes to safety. Kids can use the Ask Vince & Larry section to send in their safety questions and get expert advice. Vince and Larry tell kids what to do in tough situations such as riding a bike home when it's almost dark.

Links:

* National Highway Traffic Safety Administration
* Theater
* School Bus

Learn to live healthy—and have fun doing it

10 Tips to Healthy Eating & Physical Activity

http://ificinfo.health.org/brochure/10tipkid.htm

Eating healthy doesn't mean that kids have to eat boring foods. This site shows kids how to be healthy and still enjoy foods such as pepperoni pizza and ice cream. They just know it's smart to balance those foods with snacks such as fruits and crunchy vegetables.

Kids shouldn't waste their bodies! It's important for kids to live healthy, just like it is for adults. When kids keep their bodies happy, they'll feel better. It's easy for kids to treat their bodies right with the 10 Tips to Healthy Eating & Physical Activity. These ideas tell a young person just what to do in order to make their body a high-performance machine.

These 10 tips will really benefit kids if they are willing to work a little. They include suggestions such as starting each day with a good, healthy breakfast so the body's engine has fuel to run. Other helpful tips cover exercise pointers such as joining in physical education classes at school or playing sports to get good workouts. Each tip helps kids get started by suggesting foods that are good for them and taste great, such as bagels and spaghetti.

Kids can also take a trip to the Food Guide Pyramid by clicking on its link. There they will be able to see more secrets of healthy kids. This table shows kids how much of each type of food to eat every day (and which ones not to eat too much of!).

Any kid can make incredible things with their own hands. And any child could make their own Valentine's Day crown out of paper and candy hearts. All it takes is the right instructions to show kids how to make extraordinary crafts out of ordinary objects. Kids will never run out of ideas at the Craft Exchange. It has hundreds of ideas for all kinds of crafts. Pick a project and see how it turns out!

The Craft Exchange wants kids to work on creating things, not searching for instructions. The Exchange makes it easy to look for crafts. Look through projects sorted by months. That makes it easy to find holiday projects such as instructions for a Kids' Halloween Wreath. Every project is rated as either Very Easy, Easy, or Difficult.

The Index lists every project at the Exchange. Kids can look for crafts that use certain materials or have a certain skill level. Open the Edit menu at the top of the screen and click on Find. Then kids can type in the word they're looking for, such as "yarn" to find yarn crafts. The screen then jumps down to crafts with that word in them.

Craft projects perfect for kids of any age

CRAFT EXCHANGE

http://www.geocities.com/ EnchantedForest/3053/exchange/

There's a bunny living in every kid's washcloth! Well, maybe not yet. But when kids work on the Washcloth Bunnies project they'll make bunnies complete with wiggly eyes and a fuzzy nose. This project is easy, and the bunny makes a great nest for Easter eggs.

Links:

* Wendy's World of Crafts
* Bob's Stuff
* Bry-Back Manor

Craft Exchange

Become a magician with these simple tricks

Conjuror—Magic Tricks

http://www.conjuror.com/magictricks/

Every kid already has the magic power to repair a cut string without using tape, glue, or knots. All they have to know is the right magic trick. At this site kids will learn the right moves to fool their friends into thinking they have cut the string, even though magic just makes it look that way.

Magic tricks are amazing to watch. How can a magician tie a knot in a handkerchief with one hand? Kids can learn the secrets to this trick and others at the Conjuror site. They'll see that magic tricks don't require special powers. Each budding magician just has to practice their tricks until they get good enough to fool their friends.

The Conjuror site teaches 15 magic tricks designed for beginners. They all use items from around the house such as coins and string. That means kids don't have to worry about finding someone to saw in half! Be sure to ask Mom or Dad before trying these tricks. Some use matches or other items that can be dangerous.

Clear explanations teach kids each trick, and pictures show them how to do each move. Older kids can tackle some of the harder tricks, such as the ones using several piles of playing cards. Pay attention to the instructions that tell which card goes where! Younger kids will also find tricks they can try, like the trick of the magnetic butter knife.

Any kids who decide to become master magicians can use the site's links to learn more. It points kids to advanced tricks and stores where you can buy magic supplies.

Don't just talk about helping the environment. Do something about it! The earth is the only place we can live, so we'd better keep it nice. There are a lot of ways kids can improve water quality, wildlife habitat, and other environmental situations in their own towns. The Earth Force page tells kids how to make a difference.

Start with the Action Opps button. It describes things that kids can do to help the planet, such as riding a bike instead of getting a ride. Easy transportation alternatives like this can help cut down on air pollution. Kids can also find places in their town to plant new trees, then call up a community tree specialist who can get them planted.

Earth Force helps children understand what the big environmental problems are. This site shows that a lot of our streams are filled with bad chemicals called pollutants. Kids might be able to start a project in their neighborhood that would help cut down any existing water pollution. Any kids who do something to help raise awareness of environmental issues should write to Earth Force about it. They love to hear how kids are making things happen.

EARTH FORCE

http://www.earthforce.org/home.html

Even kids have important jobs in making the earth a better place to live. The Earth Force site teaches kids skills such as how to get people in the neighborhood involved in recycling. Help the community become more aware of environmental dangers by organizing a town meeting to find ways to help prevent any further damage.

Save a few bucks and order some of this free stuff

ABSOLUTELY FREE STUFF FOR KIDS & PARENTS

http://www.ppi-free.com/freekid.htm

Get stuff without paying anything but a little postage. The Christmas Light Ornament Kit includes a wooden ornament kids can paint. The Deputy Fire Marshal Kit provides a badge, certificate, and some stickers. Creative kids can find all kinds of great free stuff at this site.

Links:

* Free Stuff Newsletter!
* How to Suggest a Free Offer
* Free Stuff for Sewing

It's great to get something for nothing. It's also fun to get something in the mail. Get both at Absolutely Free Stuff for Kids & Parents. This big list tells kids how to order everything from information booklets to craft kits to packages of games. Just write to the mailing addresses listed on the site. It might cost a couple of dollars for shipping and handling, but kids can get a lot of neat items without spending their whole allowance.

A lot of the giveaways here are booklets for kids. Send away for the "Billy Buck Hightrail's Secret Mysterious Magical Garden" booklet to learn about eating the right foods. Other booklets help kids decide what to be when they grow up or teach fire safety. Send in for free copies of kids' magazines such as *The Turtle* and *Jack & Jill*.

Kids can order tons of free craft kits here. Some are patterns that help children make neat toys such as a bottle cap yo-yo. Other free kits have everything kids will need to make crafts such as a finger-sized mouse puppet or a stuffed penguin toy.

Click the link to the free catalogs section to order catalogs for all kinds of neat stuff.

It can be really embarrassing for kids if they don't know how to make their bed or iron clothes or even shoot a free throw. Kids can ask their parents or (oh no!) even their older brothers or sisters to show them, but that can be embarrassing too. Some kids just want to learn how to do things all by themselves.

That's where Learn2.com can help. Kids can stop here to "learn 2" do almost anything, including all the little things they've never quite figured out. It's a perfect site for curious computing kids.

Start by clicking Search. Kids can type in "make a bed," for example, and get instructions for making their bed perfectly. That'll impress their parents! Kids will learn to do each thing using the easy instructions and pictures that show them exactly what to do. This makes it easy for kids to learn something as hard as making their own paper. While kids are studying one task, Learn2.com suggests other things to learn. That way kids get smarter every time they visit.

Be sure to learn things other than boring stuff kids have to do. Learn2.com also teaches kids how to do fun activities like shooting a basketball free throw or playing checkers.

Kids learn to do almost anything all by themselves

LEARN2.COM

http://www.learn2.com

Don't get stumped by little challenges such as opening a stubborn jar lid. Learn2.com can show kids how to do it. Just run hot water over that jar. The heat makes the lid expand, making it easier to twist it right off. Then dig into whatever's inside!

Links:

* 2torial Top 10
* In The Works

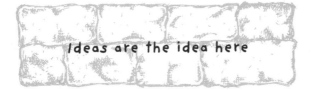

Ideas are the idea here

365 OUTDOOR ACTIVITIES

http://family.disney.com/
Categories/Activities/Features/
family_0401_01/dony/
donyout_index/

Don't
waste
another great
day sitting around
inside being bored.
Kids can try a great
outdoor activity such as
making their own bricks
from sand, straw, and flour.
They can make buildings just like
people did thousands of years ago.
That should keep energetic kids busy
for at least a day!

Ever been bored? Sometimes kids just can't think of anything to do, even when the weather's great. When Mom and Dad tell kids that it's time to get outside and do something, look here for ideas. Steve and Ruth Bennett came up with 365 great ideas for outdoor activities. That's one for every day of the year!

This site is packed with really fun ideas to keep kids busy. The ideas are divided into simple categories such as Backyard, Neighborhood, Crafts, and Imagination Games. Children will find ideas for thinking games such as drawing footprints in the dirt and having friends guess what kind of animal it is. Kids will learn to look for hidden faces in trees, walls, and other everyday objects. Youngsters on the go will also find action-packed ideas such as a volleyball game that doesn't need a net and the Ironkids contest.

A lot of these activities are so much fun that kids might enjoy them for two or three days before they even think of going back to the list to find something else to do.

Real pilots know that any piece of paper can be turned into a world-class bomber, fighter, or stunt plane. Kids just have to know where to fold the paper to make a great airplane. The Paper Airplane Hangar teaches young pilots the secrets of making paper airplanes that soar high in the sky or dart across the room.

The Hangar covers all the basics kids need to build planes like a pro. Kids will learn when to build a plane that looks good, and when to build a simple plane that can really zoom. If the planes keep crashing or zipping straight up in the air, check the tips in the solving problems section. Sometimes all that is needed is to bend the wings up a little more! Good pilots fly safely, so read the safety rules to make sure no one gets hurt during the flight.

The site has easy instructions on building four famous planes. Just follow the pictures and directions to build super fliers. The directions are some of the easiest around, so most kids should be able to build each plane with a little practice.

Use the links to find other Web sites and even some computer programs full of designs that will keep kids in the air for a long time.

Kids are cleared for takeoff! Paper airplanes rule the air here.

Paper Airplane Hangar

http://www.tycs.demon.co.uk/planes/

Kids can grab a piece of paper and start building their own air force of Classic Darts. This simple plane design is a fast flyer that anybody can build. Follow the instructions to build the plane in six steps. Then start adjusting the wings to make the Dart do special tricks.

Links:

* Science projects with paper planes
* The Paper Air Machine

Learn safety rules from real police officers

KID SAFETY ON THE INTERNET

http://www.uo.edu/oupd/ kidsafe/start.htm

Kids might know how to dial 911, but do they know what else to do if there's an accident? Look inside this police officer's notebook to see notes and pictures that teach kids safety rules for all kinds of places from the Internet to school. Keep flipping the book's pages to keep learning.

The world can seem pretty scary when kids think about all the ways they could run into trouble at school, on the sidewalk, and even online. But if children learn safety rules for all these places, they don't have to be afraid. Police officers filled the Kid Safety on the Internet site with tips to make sure kids are safe.

Click the Kid Safety button to open a slide show. Click the big arrow buttons at the bottom of the screen to turn the pages in the police officer's notebook and see the next picture. The first screen gives kids basic rules for being safe online such as being careful about talking to strangers. Other slide show pages quiz kids' safety knowledge with questions such as "Do you know what to do when you're in an accident?" The answers are always right on the next page. Some examples of other safety tips are what to do when a kid: meets strange animals, rides a bike, or faces a bully.

When finished with the Kid Safety section, check out the site's main page. The police provide great tips for topics such as kitchen safety and poisonous plants. Kids should get Mom and Dad to explore the site with them so that everyone can learn how to be safer.

Names You Know

Moving into a new place, whether it's a whole new town or just a new school, is tough. That's one problem kids won't have when they start exploring the Web. The online world might be a new one, but many of the faces on the Web are familiar.

Lots of the sites in the Names You Know section let fans get to know their favorite stars from sports, music, and movies a little better. Star Seeker, for example, has photos and facts about superstars such as Michael Jordan and Jim Carrey.

Two names kids already know are LEGO and Crayola. These building blocks have been coloring kids' imaginations for years. Now kids can see LEGO creations, tour a crayon factory, or develop ideas galore when visiting these Web pages.

Some of these sites really let kids get involved with the stars. Dr. Seuss has been famous for a long time for his funny books, but his Web site includes some new video games that let players team up with those old characters.

The stars of Disney sparkle on the Web

DISNEY'S DAILY BLAST

http://www.disney.com/Kids/ index.html

Hercules looks like a tough guy, but he wants to have some fun, too. Kids can help him join the party with the Hercules Party Pack. Everything is here to have a great Hercules party: invitations, name tags, games, and more. Kids can just print out what they need.

Fun for kids is spelled D-I-S-N-E-Y. OK, that's not really how to spell "fun," but it's safe to say Disney is the most famous name when the subject is fun for kids. Starting with the introduction of Mickey Mouse a long time ago, and more recently through movies such as *Toy Story* and *Pocahontas*, Disney has entertained several generations of kids. Now, Disney.com puts the fantastic world of Disney on the Internet.

Daily Blast on the Web is one of the latest ways to enjoy Disney. Kids pay for a Blast membership to get all of its contents, but the Blast has a lot of goodies visitors can enjoy for free, too. (Visitors can also sign up for a free 30-day membership.) The features change all the time, so it's fun to make return visits. Online comics let kids join adventures with Disney heroes such as Buzz and Woody from *Toy Story*. A new puppy's in the house, and he's terrorizing the toys! Visitors click buttons to bring up new pictures and move through the story.

Games and Activities include big-time action with Hercules, plus Disney gives away neat stuff like *101 Dalmatians* finger puppets that kids can print out. Then it's time for kids to make their own story with a puppet show!

The real Beakman knows science and a good time can go together. On TV, *Beakman's World* is packed with wacky science lessons and experiments, and the Beakman Web site is just as good. It's based on the *You Can with Beakman & Jax* cartoon strip that runs in newspapers. The Web site has the answers to science questions that kids might ask such as, "How does soap work?" Plus it lets everybody dig into science projects with demonstrations for kids to try.

Beakman's main feature is the answers to the 50 most frequently asked science questions. Beakman gives the lowdown on interesting questions such as, "Where do dreams come from?" After each answer, he describes a related experiment kids can try. One experiment teaches kids how to dream in a certain color! Nobody gets bored reading about these science topics.

The Interactive Demos are moving pictures that show how different aspects of science work. Animations illustrate a lot of neat functions such as blood flowing in the body or tiny particles in metal shifting due to magnetic attraction. Science really makes sense when Beakman explains the ideas. No wonder he's famous for making science fun!

Answers to science questions and fun experiments to try

YOU CAN WITH BEAKMAN & JAX

http://www.beakman.com

Vacation photos sometimes come from distant places, but the Hubble Space Telescope has the most far-out pictures any person's ever seen. Beakman has a few beautiful photos that the telescope took at the outer edge of what humans can see in outer space. There's even one of stars being born!

Links:

* Beakman's World on Tour
* Invention Dimension
* Cells Alive!
* The Amazing Fish Cam

Building blocks for kids' imaginations

LEGO WORLDS

http://www.lego.com/worlds.asp

Some amazing LEGO inventions are on display in the Mindstorms section, where users of the Robotics Invention System get together to talk about their cool LEGO robot creations. What other things can kids create when building with LEGOs?

Anyone who can snap two blocks together and dream up big ideas can build almost anything with LEGO blocks. Millions of these famous plastic blocks go into kids' projects around the world. But the snappable blocks are just the beginning of the amazing building tools described at the **LEGO Worlds** Web site.

On the main page, kids can click on such **LEGO** themes as Adventure World, Futuristic World, and Girls World. Clicking one of these pictures provides information about what's available from **LEGO** in that area. This is a great way to see what's new in favorite toys. Some areas have special features such as digital postcards kids can send with pictures of **LEGO** toys. There's also a cartoon story about a day at the beach with characters from the Scala **LEGO** toys for girls. Futuristic World lets young astronauts tackle an action game where they get a UFO ready for takeoff before time runs out.

The News button is the quickest path to the best entertainment **LEGO** offers online. Items listed here include some cool adventure games such as The Quest For The Ruby. On the Internet, **LEGO** has a lot of great ideas besides little blocks!

Comic strip characters may be just funny little drawings, but they're smart enough to hang out where all their fans can see them. Comic Zone is the place where some of the most famous newspaper cartoon characters make their Web home. Most newspapers don't include all these comics, but the Web hangout features popular strips such as *Luann, Marmaduke, Dilbert, Peanuts, Herman, Frank & Ernest,* and many more. Visitors can pick a strip's name from the comic list at the top of the page and dig into the funnies online.

The *Peanuts* area by itself is worth the visit. It features information on the history of the strip, profiles of characters and the artist, a chance to send digital postcards, and games like a crossword puzzle and some word games. The Timeline is an interesting way to learn about *Peanuts.* Visitors can click any date to see what Snoopy and the gang were up to at that time. When this comic strip got started way back in 1950, Snoopy sure looked different!

Editoons includes political cartoons that use pictures to talk about the news. In the United Media Store, kids can buy stuff (with their parents' permission) that features favorite characters such as *Luann* T-shirts, *Peanuts* books, and *Dilbert* dolls.

A super collection of famous comics with new strips added daily

COMIC ZONE

http://www.unitedmedia. com/comics/

The daily newspaper isn't the only place kids can check out comic strips. Some of the most popular comics are online at United Media's Comic Zone. The funny stars featured here include dogs (Marmaduke and Snoopy), cats (Fat Cats), as well as kids such as Luann and Charlie Brown.

An inside scoop on one of the best basketball teams ever

CHICAGO BULLS

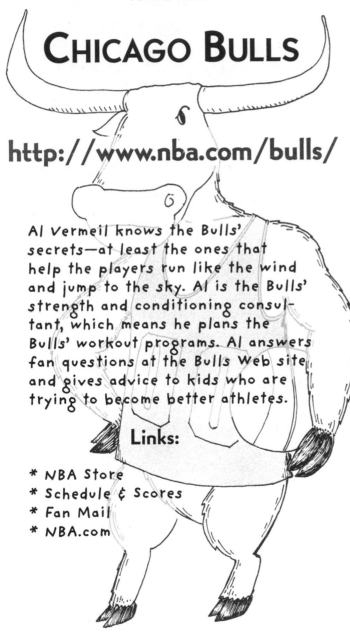

http://www.nba.com/bulls/

Al Vermeil knows the Bulls' secrets—at least the ones that help the players run like the wind and jump to the sky. Al is the Bulls' strength and conditioning consultant, which means he plans the Bulls' workout programs. Al answers fan questions at the Bulls Web site and gives advice to kids who are trying to become better athletes.

Links:

* NBA Store
* Schedule & Scores
* Fan Mail
* NBA.com

Courtside seats for Chicago Bulls basketball games are tough to get. After all, the Bulls are one of the best teams in the world, and they have the best player ever—number 23, Michael Jordan. Fortunately, the Bulls' official Web site lets fans get close to the action without fighting for a good seat. The videos, statistics, interviews, and inside facts at the Bulls site are almost as good as a visit to the Bulls locker room.

Inside The Bulls is the place to get insider information about the whole Bulls team—which includes a lot of people besides the players. This section has reports on everything from the current coaching staff to the Bulls history. Fun features cover behind-the-scenes facts such as what kinds of shoes the players wear and what an NBA championship ring looks like. Players, equipment managers, and other team members answer questions fans send through e-mail.

The Bulls Theater is loaded with action. This section has audio and video clips of the best Bulls plays. Users with the special QuickTime program can watch videos of Michael throwing down a big dunk or Toni Kukoc making a sweet pass.

The TV show listings at the Nick-elodeon site are pretty handy. They help kids find out when their favorite programs come on, so they don't miss an episode. But Nickelodeon's site has so much to do that kids just might forget about turning on the TV. All the famous Nick characters entertain visitors with games and other activities.

A backstage tour with Inside Nick shows what goes on behind the cameras. It's the place to get to know all the big stars a little better. This inside knowledge comes from people who ought to know, such as the moms of Nick stars. They share secrets about what their kids like to eat and whether they clean their rooms. Splat! has answers to the most outrageous questions sent in by kids visiting the site. Information here includes fun facts such as what junk food the stars eat while they're working. The cartoon actors are hanging around here, too. An artist shows how he draws CatDog, step-by-step.

Nick's games are some of the best on the Web. Creepy kids can compose their own ghoulish tunes with the Music Decomposer. And kids' ability to observe a situation closely is tested by Harriet The Spy. Easy instructions explain how to download each game.

A ticket to Nick news, games, activities, and more

NICKELODEON!

http://www.nick.com

Nickelodeon wants youngsters to have a blast, but it also wants them to remember to take some time for others. The Big Help link shows how concerned kids can join this project to help local communities. Kids around the whole country are working on this service project. Help your community by lending a hand!

Links:

* Write To Nick
* Nick at Nite
* Nick Jr.

Here's the best of PBS on the Net

PBS KIDS ONLINE

http://www.pbs.org/kids

All of Mister Rogers's friends in Make-Believe sure are friendly. In Mister Rogers' Children's Corner on the PBS Web site, there's a whole coloring page filled with pictures of Make-Believe neighbors showing other people how they love them. Kids have to spot all the good deeds going on.

Links:

* Charlie Horse Music Pizza
* Storytime
* Tots TV

Television fans can visit *Mister Rogers' Neighborhood*, plus *Sesame Street*, *Teletubbies* country, and *Wimzie's House* all at once. They all share an address at PBS Kids Online. This site helps kids learn more about all their favorite PBS (that stands for Public Broadcasting System) shows. With so much to do and see, this site might be even more fun than watching the shows on TV.

The main PBS site serves up a whole grab bag of fun activities. The Fun & Games link points to the games. Kid Karaoke is one of the best features of the PBS site. This online jukebox plays music and displays the words to songs on the screen. Young singers can sing along as long as they want. The Ah Ha! link on the main page leads kids to some jokes that are sure to tickle visitors' funny bones.

Sections for the shows help viewers enjoy each program more. For example, the area on *Mister Rogers' Neighborhood* explains activities kids can try that match his topics each day.

Theodore Tugboat is a strong little ship that can handle tough jobs around the harbor. But this TV star needs help with his latest adventure on the Web. Should he go make friends with the new ship in the harbor or go see what his jobs for the day will be? Should he head home or listen to a story? Readers can decide what he'll do next in the interactive stories at Theodore's Web site. Kids can read a few lines in a story, then click a link to decide Theodore's next move. The rest of the story depends on what kids choose, so they'd better give Theodore good advice!

All those decisions can be tough. When it's time to relax, there's a link to listen to a Theodore story. A friendly voice tells exciting stories about times such as the day a storm blew away Kulu the Canoe and Theodore had to rescue him. There's a new story every month. Users need the special RealAudio tool to listen to these stories. A link tells how to download it for free.

Theodore's online coloring book lets kids print out pictures of this super little boat. Kids can color the pictures and make up their own Theodore stories.

Help Theodore Tugboat with his next adventure

THEODORE TUGBOAT
ONLINE ACTIVITY CENTRE

http://www3.pbs.org/tugboat/

Instead of just watching Theodore Tugboat's adventures on TV, viewers can decide what happens in his online adventures. In one case, Theodore is lost on the ocean and can't find his harbor. Should he follow a ship he sees or go back to Blanford Buoy? Kids can tell him what to do!

Folks such as Sam-I-Am and Chief Yookeroo want visitors at Dr. Seuss' site

SEUSSVILLE

http://www.randomhouse.com/seussville/

The Cat In The Hat has e-mail, and he'll use it to answer kids' questions. They can choose to send him a question such as "Do Thing One and Thing Two have real names?" Then it's time to watch the e-mail in-box for the Cat's answer.

Even people who hate green eggs and ham will like Dr. Seuss' home on the Web. Funny characters such as Horton and the Lorax are running around his site to make sure everyone has a good time. The games and other activities are just as fun as the Dr. Seuss books the world loves to read.

It's time to play along with the greatest Dr. Seuss characters in the Games area. There's a whole group of games that takes the special Shockwave browser plug in. Onscreen instructions show how to download the special tool. Then kids can try to shoot a hoop in Elephant Ball or fix a picture in the Green Eggs And Ham Picture Scramble. Digging out a pencil gets players ready for the special collection of games that can be printed and played on paper. A maze winds to the Cat's famous hat.

There's a daily dose of wacky, wise advice in the More Fun section's daily Seussisms. Kids can also test how well they know Seuss books with the Trivia Contest. For example, where does Thidwick the Big-Hearted Moose live? If that sounds too hard, kids can relax and follow the coloring instructions for making their own Many Colored Bookmark.

Women playing pro basketball can really pop the trey or take it to the rim, and sports fans learn all about it at the WNBA's official Web site. It's *the* spot to check scores and highlights and find out what life is like for these world-class athletes.

The site has lots of videos of great WNBA action. Highlights spotlight great game moments such as some great shots from way outside and a big block from Malgorzata Dydek, who is 7'2" tall. Special audio clips demonstrate that these women have talent off the court, too. One clip shows a few stars singing in the WNBA's "Join In" TV commercial.

The Interactive section is the place to join chat sessions with WNBA stars. Fans can even vote for their own WNBA All-Star team. A special Players section helps everybody get to know the athletes. Kids can find out that Rebecca Lobo likes Road Runner cartoons and that she once went jogging with the president of the United States!

And if kids start itching to get active during their visit, the WNBA players always have some tips on how young athletes can learn to keep in shape. Who knows? Maybe the next kid who visits will play in the WNBA someday!

They got game! Dribble into this online home of the WNBA

WNBA

http://www.wnba.com

WNBA players don't just get off the couch and go play a game. They follow special warm-up and stretching routines to get their bodies ready to go to work. Young players should follow these athletes' advice about stretching so that they don't get hurt playing sports. Tips on the WNBA site demonstrate the best ways to warm up for exercise.

Links:

* Inside Stuff
* NBA.com
* Season Schedule

Science facts and experiments for kids to try

NYE LABS ONLINE

http://nyelabs.kcts.org

When objects rub together, they produce friction and slow down. Bill Nye's experiment with building a hovercraft shows how there's less friction in the air. That means things move better there. Kids can follow the instructions to build their own hovercraft and test this fact.

Links:

* The Field Museum
* MayaQuest '97
* Windows To The Universe

It seems safe to take science lessons from somebody called "The Science Guy." That's why so many kids turn to Bill Nye, the official Science Guy, to learn how things work and why things happen. Bill's lab is open to online visitors any time. The sites on this tour just might make science everybody's new favorite subject.

The Demo Of The Day is the place to look for Bill's tips on demonstrations designed for young scientists to try. Tips explain experiments such as using food coloring to show how flowers drink water. Kids can check the Demo every day to build their own series of scientific explorations.

The Episode Guide has highlights from Bill's TV shows on every topic. Stories tell a little about the show's topics, such as earthquakes, and there's an experiment on the topic to try. When Bill can't cover everything about a subject, he'll suggest places to get more information. The Web Search button points to related sites that he recommends.

The Goodies button has a collection of fun stuff like Bill Nye's photo album and the Screening Room that has video clips of Bill in action. Sounds Of Science lets everybody listen to sound clips from episodes of *Bill Nye The Science Guy.*

Video game nuts can't seem to get enough Nintendo, Sega, or PlayStation. Mom or Dad says to quit spending so much time playing games. What can the gamer do? They can go on the Web for great news and tips about the hottest games. KidsCom's GamePad area is the next best thing to actually playing video games.

GamePad offers help on games for Nintendo 64, Game Boy, Sega Genesis and Saturn, PlayStation, and a lot more. A Tip of the Week tells how to earn extra points, solve tough problems, or use codes to reveal secrets hidden in all the hottest games. The More Tips link includes a whole collection of tricks. Smart gamers drop in on the Game Talk message boards to ask game questions and give advice.

Hotshot players can take on the KidsCom Challenge. GamePad shows a tough spot in a game and challenges players to send in the strategy for getting past it. One challenge asks kids to make Yoshi celebrate in front of a melon instead of a big heart in "Yoshi's Story." Correct answers go into a drawing for special KidsKash Points that help winners earn prizes.

The hot spot to get and share video game tips

KidsCom GamePad

http://www.kidscom.com/orakc/ gamepad/index.shtml

Kids who play Quake, Sonic 3D Blast, Tetris Plus, or any other home video game, will get into the GamePad. They can drop into the Game Talk area and sound off on favorite games. Caleb, for example, says Mario Kart 64 is the best game in the universe. Kids can put their two-tokens-worth in and let other online visitors know what they think.

Links:

* KidsCom main site
* Make New Friends
* Cool Stuff

KidsCom GamePad

> Kids get tips from the pros as they learn more about baseball

BASEBALL FOR KIDS

http://www.majorleaguebaseball.com/kids/

Even little leaguers can handle the next ground ball like an All-Star. New York Yankees second baseman Chuck Knoblauch shows players how to hold the glove and set their feet. Making the next big play is just a matter of thinking of the glove as a shovel and scooping up the ball.

Let's play ball! Kids hanging around this site almost feel like pro baseball players. It offers an inside look at life as a big hitter, a star pitcher, or even the behind-the-scenes folks that make baseball games possible.

The stories here show that big-time baseball stars are real people like the people in regular families. John Halama talks about how excited he was to play Major League Baseball in his hometown. One story shows what big leaguers do when they're not playing baseball. A lot of them like to fish and golf. But some players, such as home run king Mark McGwire, love to surf the Web, just like the kids reading this book!

The pros at this site are ready to share tips on secrets of the game. Instructions explain the best way to break in a new glove. Kids can also get pointers on improving fielding and hitting skills from experts such as Tony Gwynn. Users learn that it's important to study proper stretching and warm up exercises, too.

Pro baseball involves more than just players and coaches. Stories here show that the clean-up crews and other folks work as hard as the players to make sure every baseball game is a good one.

Everybody knows a lot about Crayola crayons. After all, the average kid in North America uses up to 730 crayons by the time they're ten! That's just one of the neat facts shared at the Crayola site.

A tour of the factory shows how markers and crayons are made. Those giant barrels of wax in the pictures head through the plant and eventually become crayons. The Fun Facts section has trivia teasers on topics such as which two crayon colors are kids' favorites. The Colorful History link provides visitors with Crayola history. For instance, in 1903 they only had eight colors!

In the Coloring Book, kids can print fun pictures to color. And if kids are looking for some creative coloring ideas, the Idea Generator is just the ticket. This section helps kids come up with some really kooky coloring topics!

This site is not just about crayons. In the Craft section, kids can choose a new project to work on each week. Any kids who have cool craft ideas can send them to Crayola. Who knows? Maybe it will be added to this site's craft collection!

Tour a crayon factory to get some creative coloring ideas

CRAYOLA

http://www.crayola.com/

Crayons aren't the only fun tools Crayola makes. Their inventors keep coming up with neat ways kids can create things. The Family Play link has a lot of new ideas for creative kids. One new product for kids age five and up lets them create special treasure boxes covered with rhinestones.

Links:

* Crayola Family Play
* Tools for Fun
* Outrageous Adventures

Bunches of Beanie Babies for fans and collectors

THE OFFICIAL HOME OF THE BEANIE BABIES

http://www.beaniebabies.com

There are lots of stuffed toys. And then there are Beanie Babies. A complete list, which includes every animal Baby that has been made, shows what critters get the official seal of approval. There are pictures of all sorts of Babies, new and old, such as Bones the dog, Britannia the bear, and Canyon the cougar.

Links:

* Beanie Babies Official Club
* Beanie Connection

Everybody wants to get their hands on Beanie Babies. At least kids can find these cuddly toys on the Internet, even if they can't in real life. For the official news on Beanie Babies, come to the site posted by their maker, Ty Inc., at The Official Home of the Beanie Babies.

When fans are looking for the scoop on new Beanies, checking what's missing from their collections, or just looking to talk with other collectors, they'll find what they need at this site. The Beanie Babies Collection page gives the name and picture of every animal. All of the cute, cuddly collectibles are here, from Erin the bear to Web the spider. Kids can add up how many of these they have.

It looks like these online Babies aren't just ordinary toys. Some of the animals keep diaries and put them on the Web site. Kids can read about how the Babies keep busy every day doing things like playing games and visiting friends.

Anyone can sign up for a free Beanie Connection membership and share messages with other fans. Members can talk about everything from what price is right for a new doll to what their favorite Beanie is and why.

Michael Jordan's here. So is Hanson. Even Will Smith's here. In fact, this fan site is *the* place to check up on all the favorite sports heroes, movie stars, and entertainers. Fans can even find out about the movies, TV shows, and albums themselves. The people running Star Seeker make sure that only the best celebrity links get in. That way this site always has the best resources for news, photos, and cool information about the stars.

The main page makes it easy to find a favorite star. Star Seeker sorts sites into easy-to-use categories such as Music, TV, Movies, Movie Stars & Other Celebs, and Sports. Finding a star is as easy as clicking one of these categories and then choosing other categories to find the right topic. Kids can click Movie Stars & Other Celebs, for example, then click Cartoons. They'll see listings of sites for all kinds of cartoon heroes such as Batman, Garfield, Popeye, and the X-Men.

The categories let fans quickly find just the right information. If a fan wants to know when their favorite band's next album will come out, they can use the Music section to find sites about groups such as Hanson, The Spice Girls, or the Backstreet Boys.

Celebrities, pop stars, sports heroes—find facts about kids' favorites here

STAR SEEKER

http://www.starseeker.com/

The big stars are easy to reach here. Fans may not meet their sports, music, and entertainment heroes, but they can learn more about them at the Star Seeker site. There are fun facts, photos, and inside gossip about famous folks kids might have only seen on TV or heard on the radio before.

Links:

* Hot Movies
* Pick Of The Week

This site will keep young readers turning the pages

JUST FOR KIDS WHO LOVE BOOKS

http://www.geocities.com/Athens/Olympus/1333/kids.htm

Using Web sites about books can be as fun as reading the books themselves. For example, kids who love the Little House book series can visit this site for links to pictures of the real Laura Ingalls Wilder. Her picture might look different from what's in a reader's imagination!

Links:

* Authors
* Titles and Series

Scary books, country books, animal books, fairy tale books. They're all covered here at a site that helps kids find out more about their favorite books. A friendly librarian from Canada built this site to help young readers. The big list of links points to sites about great kids' books all over the World Wide Web.

The left side of the screen holds all the links. These list names of authors, titles of books, and names of book series. Visiting a site about a favorite author or book is as easy as clicking a link. Book links include titles from series such as The Baby-sitters Club, the Little House books, Goosebumps, and Winnie The Pooh.

The site for every book is different, so exploring a lot of them doesn't get boring. Most of the sites include pictures, such as those from the Goosebumps television show. Other sites list all the books that have been written by an author. This helps fans of certain authors decide what book to read next. Sometimes a book site has audio and video clips. All these links are great ways for kids to get more fun out of the books they like to read.

Multimedia Resources

It's a movie screen. It's a radio. It's a picture gallery. It's a . . . computer? Computers can be all of these things when they're connected to the right multimedia sites on the Web. The word "multimedia" describes stuff that comes from computers besides plain words. The Web is packed with multimedia features that make using a computer a lot of fun.

Multimedia users might start using the TV and radio less and the computer more. Sites such as Broadcast.com play CDs and signals from radio stations right through the computer. It's like having a personal jukebox! It takes a couple of special programs to use all this stuff, but each site explains what's needed and where to find it for free.

It only takes a few seconds to look up all kinds of photos at The Amazing Picture Machine. Other sites, such as the ZooNet Image Archives, have pictures of one thing—animals. Add some wild sound effects from sites like SoundAmerica, and the computer becomes a real fun house of sights and sounds!

Listen to CDs or radio stations from around the world

BROADCAST.COM

http://www.broadcast.com

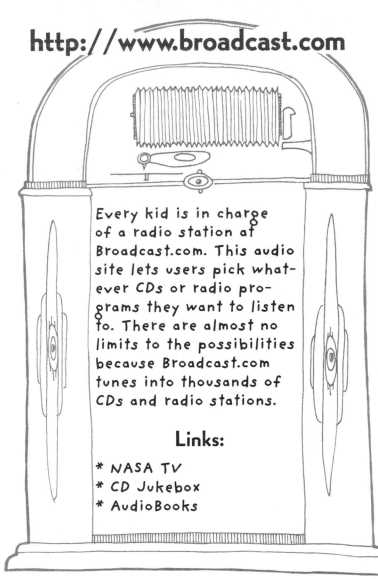

Every kid is in charge of a radio station at Broadcast.com. This audio site lets users pick whatever CDs or radio programs they want to listen to. There are almost no limits to the possibilities because Broadcast.com tunes into thousands of CDs and radio stations.

Links:

* NASA TV
* CD Jukebox
* AudioBooks

Computers become the world's strongest radios when they're tuned into the Broadcast.com site. This cool site brings in broadcasts of music, sports, and talk shows from around the world. It's a blast listening to a radio station broadcasting live from the other side of the country. It's like taking a trip without leaving the house. Another feature is the CD jukebox. It's filled with thousands of CDs that users can listen to. What a great way to hear the latest album from your favorite band!

Sites such as Broadcast.com are really on the cutting edge. Soon, people might even trade in their radios for computers! To use Broadcast.com a computer needs the RealPlayer program. Parents can find it for free at the company's Web site (http://www.real.com).

Special features tune the computer into programs such as lectures from educational conferences or audio books where someone reads stories out loud. There are even live TV channels where kids can watch exciting events such as the space shuttle blasting off. The picture reception isn't as good as on TV, but this feature is still worth checking out.

Most of history passed by before anyone could take pictures or movies of it. Photographic cameras hadn't been invented when Egyptians built the pyramids, and there weren't any TV cameras around to film battles in the War of 1812. Fortunately, kids studying space travel don't have that problem. Cameras have been around to takes pictures of all the rockets and astronauts humans have sent into outer space. The Galactic Odyssey Web site has put a lot of these photos and movies online. The collection is an awesome way to see the people and machines that have explored space.

The video gallery is loaded with movies. Kids need to get the free plug-in, QuickTime (http://www.apple.com/quicktime/), to watch the films. The movies cover everything from man's first step on the moon to images of the space shuttle blasting off on a mission. The photos of rockets are a bit fuzzy, but they offer a peek at the machines that carry people away from earth.

It's easy to read the stories behind the pictures thanks to the information on rocketry, pioneers of space travel, and medical advances made through space exploration. There are also pictures of famous scientists such as Albert Einstein and Isaac Newton.

See pictures of scientists, astronauts, and space ships that are out of this world

GALACTIC ODYSSEY

http://library.advanced.org/11348/
#Video Gallery

Sometimes getting out of bed can be pretty tough. Imagine trying to climb off the entire earth! That's what the space shuttle has to do to reach outer space. Films of the shuttle blasting off show what monstrous engines it takes to shoot a rocket off of the earth.

Links:

* NASA
* Medical Advances
* Your Space Prediction

Take an online safari and study pictures of wild animals

ZooNet Image Archives

http://www.mindspring.com/ ~ zoonet/gallery.html

How do anteaters get at all those tasty insects they love to eat? It's easy to learn how with ZooNet's picture of this animal's long snout—made just for sucking up tiny crawling creatures! All kinds of pictures at this site offer close-up views for studying how wild animals really look.

Links:

* Birmingham Zoo Gallery
* Jackson Zoo Gallery
* Primate Gallery
* ZooSpell

Some animal watchers have to crouch in hot, sticky jungles or cold, windy mountains to get a glimpse of wild creatures. Smart Web users know there's a better way to get a close-up look at animals. They just visit the ZooNet Image Archives site for pictures of hundreds of different creatures from around the world. The pictures are great, and nobody has to worry about getting chomped by a polar bear or trampled by a rhinoceros!

Users can find pictures of almost any animal by scrolling down the page to the Animal Pictures section. It has links to collections of photos organized by types of animals such as Birds and Fowl, Carnivores, Monkeys and Apes, and Rodents. Within each section, finding a picture is as easy as clicking an animal's name. Most of these color pictures are very clear, and the fangs on a cougar or the feathers on a swan seem to jump off the screen. There are several different shots of the animals. For instance, kids can see a giraffe in both walking and resting positions.

Clip art is kind of like a book of stickers on a computer. Kids can peel regular stickers off a page and stick them wherever they want. Clip art works almost the same way. Users just take one of the clip art drawings off a Web site and put it wherever they want on a computer. The drawings come in handy for school reports, as pictures on the computer screen, or even to hang on the wall when they're printed out on a color printer.

Yahooligans! Downloader is the ultimate clip art browser. This page lists some of the best sites that have free clip art on the Web. One of the best is the ClipArt Collection. This site lists images by topics that kids are familiar with such as animals, cartoons, maps, and music. The How-To section on the main page explains everything kids need to know in order to save, import, or print pictures. There is also a window on the Downloader site that lets kids search for any image that they are trying to find.

This site doesn't stop with just clip art though. Kids can also get a lot of animated pictures as well. These are pictures that actually move. Animations can really add life to any computer document but are especially cool for young Web page designers to use on their site.

Free pictures to use, freely, wherever kids choose

YAHOOLIGANS! DOWNLOADER

http://www.yahooligans.com/ Downloader/Pictures/Clip_Art/

It's easy to add an individual touch to school reports with help from Yahooligans! Downloader. This site has lots of links to free pictures of funny little arrows, light bulbs, and all kinds of stuff. When the report is printed, the drawings will really help ideas stick out on the paper.

SOUND SAFARIS

http://www.wildsanctuary.com/safari.html

It would be cool to hear the sounds an alligator makes in his home in the swamp. But a real alligator might eat somebody before they got a chance to hear his sounds! This Web site can play the gator's sounds while kids stay a safe distance away from this snaggle-toothed reptile.

Links:

* Wild Sanctuary Main Page
* Antarctic Journal
* Gift Shop

Anybody can use a computer to call up some animals around the world and hear what they're saying. Well, people can't really call animals. But the Sound Safaris Web site lets users hear recordings of what all kinds of animals are saying. A few animals are angry, some are looking for friends, and some just want to keep everybody away from their homes.

A map of the world appears on the main page of this Web site. Kids just point to the part of the world that they want to visit. Tours head to places such as North America, South America, Africa, and even Antarctica. North America features animals such as a rattlesnake and a walrus. Clicking the Listen button plays a sound clip of the walrus clacking its teeth and the rattlesnake making its scary rattling sound. That means it's smart to stay away!

The text next to each picture explains how and why each animal makes its sound. For instance, a rattlesnake's rattle is made of the same kind of stuff as a person's fingernails; lemurs shriek to tell other lemurs, "Stay off my turf!"; and seals make sounds that can be heard up to 15 miles away underwater. Any kids who still feel wild after visiting this site can check out the Sound Safari links.

Surfing the World Wide Web always sounds like fun. But the SoundAmerica Web site helps computers really make some noise with its clips from famous cartoons, movies, television shows, and wacky sound effects that make everybody laugh. This is one site that definitely sounds like a good time.

Each section lists the clips available. When users click one, they'll have to wait a few seconds while the clip loads up. Some of the sound effects are gross, like the barfing noise or the big belch. Others are just funny ones like the "boing" sound cartoons use a lot or the mooing cows. The Cartoons section has clips from lots of kids' favorite funny characters. There's a clip of Scooby Doo laughing. There's even Elmer Fudd talking about how he'll finally get that "scwewy wabbit."

All of these sound clips are fun to listen to at the site. Plus, kids can download them to their computer and hear the Tasmanian Devil or Porky Pig whenever they feel like it.

It sounds like there's a TV inside the computer

SOUNDAMERICA
http://www.soundamerica.com

"The Animaniacs" are ready to come over for a visit. Well, at least it sounds like they're visiting. SoundAmerica has sound clips from this cartoon and more. It's fun to surprise friends by making a computer talk just like Dot or the Warner Brothers.

Links:
* Soundspace
* Cartoons Wavs
* Sound Gallery

A friendly bear shares art with his visitors

BILLY BEAR 4KIDS.COM

http://www.billybear4kids.com

Teddy bears and tigers are loose on the computer screen! A special screen saver from Billy Bear puts pictures of animals, toys, and other fun things on the screen whenever users leave the computer alone for a while. They run around the screen until someone moves the mouse to make them disappear.

Links:

* Animal Scoop
* StoryBooks
* Show & Tell

Billy Bear likes to help kids. So he built this Web site and stuffed it full of cool things kids can use, such as drawings and moving pictures for the computer screen. Billy Bear's pictures are "clip art." That means users can take them off his site and use them for projects or maybe to decorate the computer screen.

Billy lets everyone choose what packages of pictures to take. His regular clip art collections have all kinds of fun drawings of things such as ice cream cones, bears, alligators, and street signs. He also has packages of drawings for holidays such as Christmas and Easter.

He has lots of other tools for making computers more interesting, too. Billy Bear's screen savers can really dress up kids' monitors. Screen savers put pictures on the screen after the computer hasn't been used for a while. Then, when someone comes back to use the computer, they might be greeted by a sun telling them that they did their best today (or whatever else you decide to use)! Instructions for using the screen savers are on the Web site. Parents can read the instructions and help set up the screen savers.

Cartoons aren't only on TV and in movies. They're right on the computer screen for the visitors of Cartoon World. This super cartoon hangout has sounds, video clips, pictures, and even some games from kids' favorite cartoons.

The World's Greatest link points to some of the all-time favorite characters. Check out the video clips of characters from *The Lion King* such as Simba and Pumba. Big stars such as Winnie The Pooh and The Flintstones have their pictures on this site. Look down the page for songs from shows such as *The Jetsons* and *Inspector Gadget*. Click the links and sing along!

Fans of adventure and action cartoons can find goodies here, too. There are sounds and video clips from *Voltron, Johnny Quest, He-Man, The Transformers,* and *The Thundercats*. Some cartoons have special features such as coloring book pages featuring characters from *Scooby Doo.*

One of the best areas at Cartoon World is under the Fun & Games button on the main page. The challenge is to identify cartoon characters just by their shadows.

Sufferin' succotash! It's Cartoon World!

CARTOON WORLD

http://www.cet.com/~rascal/welcome.html

With a sly look and a "beep-beep," Road Runner dashes away from the coyote. He-Man's telling the story of Castle Grayskull's Power. Scooby Doo's laughing himself silly through a mystery. The best part is, they're doing all of this on the computer. It's easy to get up close and personal with cartoon stars at Cartoon World.

Links:

* Starblazers
* Saturday Morning Live
* Mystery
* Action

Get down while learning with Schoolhouse Rock

SCHOOLHOUSE ROCK

http://genxtvland.simplenet.com/SchoolHouseRock/index-hi.shtml

There's never been a planet that Interplanet Janet hasn't seen. Her cartoon teaches about all the places in outer space she's visited. Her song about how Mars is red and Saturn has rings is a popular Science Rock song. Check out Janet and the rest of the gang here for lots of rockin' good times.

Links:

* Events
* Products
* About This Site

Sometimes it's easier to learn things by singing. The right tune can help kids learn math, history, and even grammar. That's what makes Schoolhouse Rock so much fun. These musical cartoons have been playing on Saturday mornings since before most kids were born, and they've helped millions of kids to learn. Now everybody can watch the cartoons whenever they want, thanks to the Schoolhouse Rock Web site.

At the site's main page, visitors pick an area to learn about such as Grammar Rock, Multiplication Rock, America Rock, or Scooter Computer & Mr. Chips. Inside each area, kids can choose an episode of *Schoolhouse Rock* to listen to or watch. Hits here include "Conjunction Junction," "No More Kings," and "Naughty Number Nine." After watching these a couple of times, kids will be able to multiply any number by nine! Kids will have to make sure that they have RealAudio and QuickTime on their computers in order to hear the sounds and watch the cartoons.

There are enough cartoons here to keep kids learning for a long time. Visitors should check out the story of where *Schoolhouse Rock* came from and the TV listing so you can catch the Rock on TV on Saturdays.

Schoolhouse Rock

The old story about "Alice In Wonderland" tells of a little girl's adventures in a strange place where cats disappear and rabbits carry watches. Readers can jump into this weird world at the Alice's Adventures in Wonderland site. They can read the book online, but this site has more to offer than just a book. It's full of surprises such as drawings that move (and even talk) when least expected.

Things start, of course, with the first chapter. Pretty music plays as visitors read about how Alice chases a strange white rabbit down a hole. Before long, she falls deep in the hole and winds up looking at a bottle labeled "Drink Me." Did she drink what was in the bottle? Visit the site to find out and then join her for the rest of her wild adventures.

It's easy to get caught up in the story. Alice talks as she explores Wonderland. And that weird little rabbit even winks and runs away when readers look at the pictures. It's almost like being in Wonderland! Everyone should try typing a message to Alice by clicking Chat With Alice on the main page. She answers the messages kids type.

Follow the White Rabbit with Alice and travel down a virtual rabbit hole

ALICE'S ADVENTURES IN WONDERLAND

http://www.megabrands.com/alice/goalice.html?

Alice is in a strange spot this time. She's stuck in a court trial with characters such as the Mad Hatter and King of Hearts. She's growing back to her regular full size, and she's just been called as a witness in the trial! Find out what happens next by reading the story at the Web site.

An inside tour of a cartoon studio

WARNER BROS.

ANIMATION MUSIC & SOUND EFFECTS

http://www.wbanimation.com/cmp/ani8.htm

A Foley artist's whole job is to make wacky noises. These folks watch cartoons and make the sounds such as stomping feet, whizzing rocks, and slamming doors to go with the pictures. Listen to the sounds and learn something along the way at the Warner Bros. Web site.

Links:

* Warner Bros. Animation page
* Bonus.com

Now any kid can use those wacky sounds heard in favorite cartoons. This site lets everyone download skidding sounds and whistles to liven things up around the computer. But the sound effects here are just a small part of the cartoon resources. The Music & Sound Effects pages are just one chapter in Animation 101. This cartoon school goes behind the scenes to see how studios make cartoons. It's amazing how many adults it takes to make one cartoon.

The fun animation "course" teaches students how favorite cartoons such as *The Animaniacs* grow from an idea in a writer's brain to the show kids see on television. Kids can follow the whole course or use links on the main page to skip to the parts that sound interesting.

Artwork includes the first sketches of Babs and Buster Bunny. It takes a lot of sketches and coloring to make a cartoon. Pictures on the site show people called Foley artists crawling on the ground to make sounds like horses galloping. By the time the course is over, students will know a lot more about those sound clips, and they'll understand how the sounds really came from people, not a cartoon character.

The World Wide Web is like the world's largest photo album. It has pictures of everything from aardvarks to zeppelins. The Amazing Picture Machine helps users find the pictures they need in this giant library of photos. Just type the name of a person, place, or thing, and the Picture Machine will point out where to find the pictures. This is the perfect tool for finding pictures for fun or photos to liven up school reports on people, machines, animals, or anything else.

Visitors just type in the name of what they're looking for and click the Start Search button. Searching for "giraffe," for example, finds pictures of giraffes hanging out in the trees. Descriptions tell all about each picture, whether it's color or black-and-white, and some technical stuff such as how big it is. A clickable link brings up the picture. When kids find a picture they like, they can click it with their right mouse button and choose Save Picture As to save it on the computer's hard drive. It's smart to check each Web site to make sure the pictures' owners don't mind people using them.

THE AMAZING PICTURE MACHINE

http://www.ncrtec.org/picture.htm

Most people can't go to every place on earth to shoot snapshots. However, the Amazing Picture Machine Web site lets people take a look at tons of photos from all over. See Egyptian pyramids, African lions, or gigantic whales swimming in the ocean—all in an hour!

Glossary

Archive. An electronic attic for storing old information such as articles from old issues of an online magazine or questions already answered by a homework expert. Many Web sites put out new information all the time, but they save all the old information in an archive.

Bookmark. A Web browser tool that makes it easy to find sites the user likes again and again. The user, when visiting a site they like, marks it with a bookmark. They then choose the Bookmarks option in their Web browser to see a list of all the sites they've bookmarked. Click one to visit the site. Also called Favorites in some Web browsers.

Browser. Computer software that lets users visit Web sites. Microsoft Internet Explorer and Netscape Navigator are the most popular Web browsers. Browsers are the places where users click buttons, links, and pictures to move around in Web sites.

CD-ROM. A disc that looks just like a music compact disc (CD) but stores computer programs. Almost all software now comes on CD-ROMs, and many people call software "CD-ROMs."

Chat. An Internet feature that lets users type messages that appear on a friend's screen as soon as they type them. When several people get together to chat, they're in a "chat room." It's almost like having a real-life conversation, except users read what others say on the screen instead of hearing it.

Clip Art. Pictures people take off the Web to use however they want. If someone was writing a school report and needed a picture of a monkey, they could visit a clip art Web site and look for a picture of a monkey. When they found one, kids could download it and use it in their report. Clip art gets its name because the pictures used to be on paper, and people "clipped" them out of a book and pasted them onto other papers.

Copyright. A legal rule that says people own what they create. If someone draws a picture, they can copyright it; that means no one else can use that picture without their permission. Users can't use copyrighted pictures, sounds, or movies without permission from whomever created them. Make sure a Web site grants permission for people to use its pictures before downloading them.

Download. Taking pictures, sounds, programs, or other information off the Internet and putting it on the user's computer.

E-mail. An Internet feature that lets people send typed messages to friends. It's like mailing a regular letter, except the message is electronic and travels quickly over the Internet. E-mail can go around the world in less than five minutes! Users can attach files, such as pictures and sound clips, to e-mail messages.

FAQs. Frequently Asked Questions. Lists of FAQs answer the questions people usually have when they first visit a site, such as "Where did you get the name for this site?" Check out FAQs to figure out what's going on when first arriving at a site.

Favorites. *See* Bookmarks.

HTML. HyperText Markup Language. The programming language used to create Web pages. A lot of programs exist now that use HTML and make creating Web pages easier.

Hyperlink. Words on a Web site that users can click to visit another Web page. Hyperlinks, called "links" for short, are usually underlined and appear in a different color.

Interactive. A Web site or computer program that lets the user enter information or control what happens on the screen. One kind of interactive Web site might let someone solve a puzzle by moving blocks around the screen with their mouse.

Internet. A network that connects computers around the world. When a computer is connected to the Internet, that computer's user can access stories, pictures, sounds, movies, and all kinds of other nformation other Internet users have put out there for them to see. It's like exploring new places, except the information travels over telephone lines and through a computer.

Java. A special programming language that runs little programs on Web pages. Sometimes the games kids play at a Web site use Java.

Modem. A part inside of the computer (or sometimes outside) that lets the computer connect to a telephone line and talk with other computers around the world. A computer using a modem is making a phone call just like people do, except its conversations bring up Web pages and transfer e-mail instead of spoken conversations.

Mouse. A handheld tool used to point to things on a computer screen. Point the arrow on the screen to something and click the mouse button by pressing and releasing it. Some mouses have a right-hand button that provides more functions.

Multimedia. Any kind of information on the computer screen other than plain words. Multimedia includes pictures, sounds, and movies.

Password. A secret word people use to get into Web sites that only let their members in. When users join some Web clubs, they'll get to make up a password, and then use it every time they visit the Web site.

RealAudio. A special program users can add to their Web browser in order to listen to recorded sounds and music online. RealAudio lets users try out songs on CDs they're thinking of buying or hear sound clips from their favorite movies. RealAudio can be downloaded for free, and it's easy to add to the browser.

RealPlayer. This is just like RealAudio, except it also lets users watch movies online.

Scanner. A device that turns regular pictures and printed stuff into information on a computer screen. It is kind of like a photocopier, but instead of making copies, it makes electronic images of the original.

Screen Saver. A picture that comes up on a computer screen if the user hasn't used the computer for a while. Screen savers got their name because old monitors could be damaged if one image stayed on the screen too long. Screen savers put changing pictures up that "saved" the screen from damage. Now screen savers are just for fun, and a lot of them are available on the Internet for kids to download for free.

Search Engine. A Web site that helps users find information online. People can go to a search engine such as Yahooligans! and type in the words "the Simpsons" to get a list of all the sites out there with information on that cartoon. A search engine is like the card catalog at the library; it is the best place to start looking for information.

Shockwave. A special program users can add to their Web browser so they can view animations such as cartoons and play lots of games. When visiting a site with features that need Shockwave, a message will let you know. Users can download Shockwave for free.

Site. The name for a collection of Web pages on one topic put up by one person or group. When visiting pages put up by somebody named Bob, all the pages Bob put on the Internet are part of his Web site.

Surfing. The word for cruising around the Internet, looking for information. When people get done working online, they'll say something like, "I've been surfing the Net for two hours."

URL. Uniform Resource Locator. The fancy name for a Web page's address. Things like "http://www.nickelodeon.com" are URLs.

User. Computer user. This is the name for people when they are "using" their computers.

Virtual. A word that describes Internet versions of things found in real life. A virtual postcard isn't a real postcard you drop in the mail; it's an electronic message that people can send. A virtual zoo may be an online collection of pictures of animals in a real zoo somewhere.

World Wide Web. The easy-to-use part of the Internet that includes pictures and lots of buttons people can click. Most of the time users are online, they'll be working with the Web.

Yahoo! One of the most famous and easiest to use Web search engines. Yahoo! is a free service and lets users type in words to search for on the Web. It also organizes sites into categories such as "Travel" and "Music."

index